Steve Cameron

GATE
11
BYU

WILD BLUE YONDER

The High Flying Story of BYU Football

by Dick Harmon and Steve Cameron

Foreword by Ty Detmer

Photography by Mark Philbrick

Addax Publishing Group

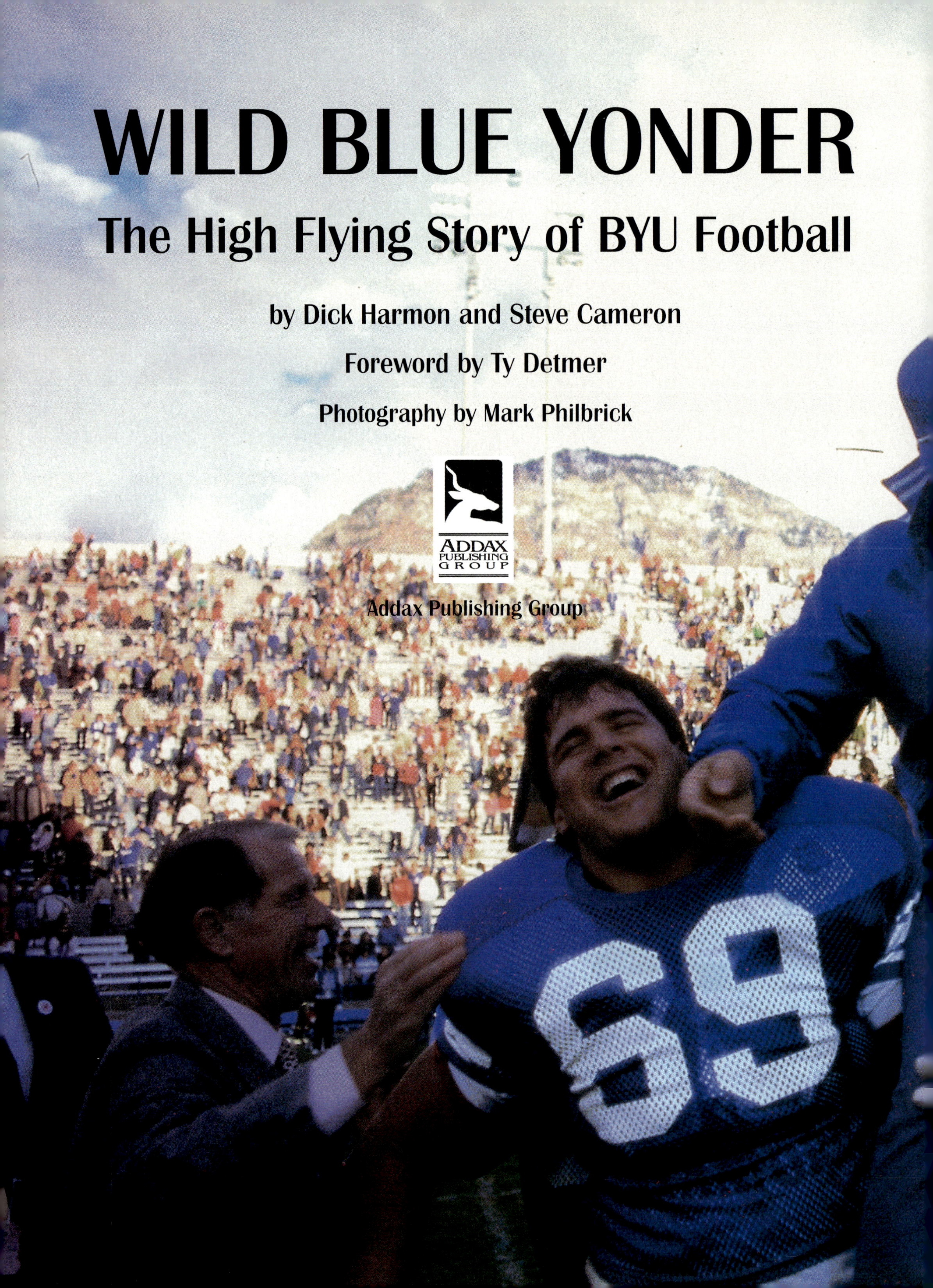

BYU
BYU

Published by Addax Publishing Group

Photo Editor: Mark Philbrick
Design and Typography by Anita Stumbo
Cover Design by Jerry Hirt
Dust Jacket and Authors' photos by Brian Winter
Contributing photographers: Brian Winter and Marc Lester
Select photos courtesy Brigham Young University

Addax Publishing Group
8643 Hauser Drive · Suite 235
Lenexa, Kansas 66215

ISBN: 1-886110-33-6

Distributed to the trade by:
Andrews McMeel
4520 Main Street
Kansas City, Missouri 64111

Printed in the United States of America

1 3 5 7 9 10 8 6 4 2

Library of Congress Cataloging-in-Publication Data

Harmon, Dick, 1952–
Wild Blue Yonder: The High Flying Story of BYU Football/by Dick Harmon and Steve Cameron.
p. cm.
ISBN 1-886110-33-6
1. Brigham Young University—Football—History. 2. Brigham Young Cougars (Football team)—History. I. Cameron, Steve. II. Title.
GV958.B75H37 1997 97-38348
796.332'63'0979224—dc21 CIP

For our families, who hung in there and helped out so much during the hectic times.

DICK HARMON has been covering BYU football and a myriad of other sports for two decades for *The Daily Herald* in Provo. The author of successful biographies of former Cougar stars Steve Young and Ty Detmer, Harmon also is a regular contributor to several national magazines.

Longtime member of the Football Writers Association of America and Heisman Trophy voter, Harmon publishes a weekly newletter on BYU sports and contributes to various computer on-line services.

Harmon lives with his wife, AnnaLee, and three children in Orem, Utah.

STEVE CAMERON is a career newspaper and radio journalist who is now sports editor of *The Daily Herald.* Cameron is the author of nine books, including "Huck Finn Grows Up," the story of Green Bay quarterback Brett Favre. Cameron's anecdotal chronicle of his 30 years in sports, *If Bobby Knight Thinks I'm a Moron, How Can I Be All Bad?* also is being released in 1997 by Addax Publishing Group.

Editor of a golf guide to the Caribbean which was published in 1983, Cameron has hosted sports talk shows in several major markets and contributes to *Inside Sports* and other magazines.

Cameron resides in Pleasant Grove, Utah, with his wife Sylvia, and their family.

Contents

SMITH

BYU

Acknowledgments

AS ENJOYABLE AND REWARDING as it might be to see a book like this through to its conclusion, it's still a lot of work and it depends on the help and faith of so many people.

Our thanks, first of all, to everyone at Brigham Young University—including president Merrill Bateman, vice president R.J. Snow, athletic director Rondo Fehlberg and his able assistants Pete Witbeck and Val Hale, sports information director Ralph Zobell along with his entire staff, and of course, coach LaVell Edwards and all those great folks in the BYU football program.

Mark Philbrick, the university's official photographer, served as photo editor on this project and deserves a deep bow, along with contributing photographer Brian Winter of *The Daily Herald* in Provo.

We are tremendously grateful, obviously, that Ty Detmer took time away from his day job quarterbacking the Philadelphia Eagles to write a Foreword.

Much appreciation, as well, to publisher Kirk Parkinson and editor Mike Patrick of *The Daily Herald* for allowing us the time to wrestle with this thing . . . and to our colleagues at the paper for their help, advice and good humor.

Some of the information we used came from two outstanding books by Lee Benson: *LaVell: Airing It Out* and *They Came to Pass.*

Naturally, we also gleaned a lot of material from newspaper and magazine stories about BYU football. Those sources are too numerous to mention here, but we hope our colleagues—past and present—will accept our nod for a job well done.

Thanks a thousand times over to family and friends who offered encouragement and kindness when we needed long hours, days and weeks to drive this book the length of the field.

For AnnaLee Harmon and Sylvia Cameron, no words are enough. Without you, it couldn't have happened.

Kudos, too, to the very patient Bob Snodgrass of Addax Publishing Group, who brought this concept to life and then put it into print.

And finally, our deepest gratitude to those remarkable people who made this project possible in the first place: the players, coaches and support staff who have turned BYU football into such an amazing success story.

We sincerely hope we've done you justice.

—DICK HARMON
STEVE CAMERON
Provo, Utah
August 1997

Foreword

by Ty Detmer

TRYING TO DESCRIBE BYU football and this book in just a few words is no easy task. I definitely had a great time playing at BYU. It gave me a great foundation for what I am doing today, playing in the NFL.

It was a lot of fun, full of exciting times. The experience I had at BYU is what playing college football is all about. If I had to do it again, I'd do the same thing all over again.

As a quarterback taking the reins of the BYU passing offense, you find yourself with a unique opportunity. Many people these days talk about the West Coast offense and how it's a quarterback's dream, but the BYU offense incorporated all of those things. In fact, it's similar to what we do with the Philadelphia Eagles—definitely quarterback friendly.

For quite awhile now, playing football at BYU has meant playing winning football.

It's a combination of many things. The consistency of the coaching staff is a big part of it. In the latter years under LaVell Edwards, the staff has stayed around and worked together. They've added new wrinkles here and there, adjusting to the new defenses that come along.

The consistency of the program is amazing. While I was there, we lost only one home game—against Washington State.

It's a great place to play. I don't know what it is, but BYU doesn't lose at home very often and there's really a great atmosphere there.

The win over Miami in Provo is a game people still come up to me and talk about. It was exciting, perhaps one of the most exciting I've played because of who they were—ranked No. 1 at the time and defending national champions.

We have a couple of guys with the Eagles who were on that Miami team, linebacker Darin Smith and receiver Chris T. Jones. Whenever they start talking about playing at Miami, I remind them of the day they came to Provo. You can't describe the feeling of being in that intense game, putting everything you have into it, then coming out with a win.

These memories of playing college football in Provo are the kind you never forget.

One of the inspiring things about BYU football is the success they've had over the years with talent which would be considered less than teams that are consistently ranked up high. This says a lot about BYU and what can be done when teams come together and work together.

I don't think BYU puts the most talent on the field, week in and week out. But when the Cougars come on the field, everyone is on the same page, of one mind and purpose.

When you have that, a lot gets done.

A great example of this was the Green Bay Packers, Super Bowl champions in 1996–97. I started my pro career with the Packers, and I think it's fair to say they may not have had the most talent in the NFL when they won the Super Bowl.

If you look at the teams they were playing against, the Packers didn't spend the most money on guys. But they played together. They were guys who had been in the system together and knew what to do.

BYU is the collegiate version of that situation.

At BYU, you have a timing offense, so people have to be together and the longer they work together, the better they are. The thing about BYU is that the team will always do better than an opponent that has five or six great players and tries to let them make all the plays.

Football is a team game, and when 11 guys on the field are working together, that's a tough combination to beat. That's how it's been at BYU—team football. It's a compliment to the coaching staff and the system. LaVell Edwards is very consistent and honest with the players. Being consistent is important because you can't lead a team by being one way on a certain day, and then change and treat people differently another day.

Coach Edwards takes care of the players and makes sure they do what they're supposed to do. There are times people step out of line, just like anywhere, but he deals with it.

When you first come in, you see Coach Edwards as a very serious, businesslike guy, and you might be intimidated because he never seems to smile. But the more you're around him, the more you enjoy being around him and playing for him.

We used to meet and hang around outside his office. We even ate lunch sitting in the lobby of the office—talking, visiting and reading newspapers with the secretaries.

There are a lot of programs where you can't go into the coaches' offices. It's like sacred ground or something, and you aren't welcome there unless you're summoned or ordered to make an appearance. It's like a business office at some places.

But even now, when I go back to BYU, guys are hanging around eating lunch or studying right outside of coach Edwards' office door. It's a great atmosphere.

When I walked on campus for the first time, I never in my wildest imagination thought I would someday win the Heisman Trophy. I just hoped I'd get a chance to play football. That king of thing just happens.

What happened to me, I've said many times, was the culmination of efforts by many people.

Quarterbacks like Gary Shiede, Gifford Nielsen, Marc Wilson, Jim McMahon, Robbie Bosco and Steve Young paved the way, and BYU became known as a quarterback factory. When I came, all I did was take advantage of what had transpired before me.

Ty Detmer

They'd all come close before. I was in the right place at the right time, with a good team that always pulled together. But other people put BYU on the map.

This book tells the BYU football story in a simple, but direct way. The pictures capture some of the big moments and the spirit of what has to be one of the most exciting college football programs anywhere. It was thrill to be part of it. It still is.

—TY DETMER

From The Athletic Director... -Rhondo Fehlberg

I first met publisher Bob Snodgrass and author Steve Cameron two years ago in Fort Collins, Colorado where BYU was preparing for a football game against Colorado State. They had collaborated on a number of successful books about great personalities and traditions in the world of sports and wanted to explore the possibility of doing a similar publication about BYU football. They explained that many of the ingredients that had made their other books successful existed in Provo: a history of success, strong traditions, larger-than-life personalities, strong indicators of future success, and a large group of interested fans and public who would want such a publication in their libraries, offices and homes.

Their enthusiasm was contagious. As we paged through their commemorative volumes about teams, it became easy to visualize page after page of the story that has become one of the most compelling in all of college football. The humble beginnings — those lean years and decades of frustration and futility. The coming of LaVell Edwards — that matter of fact, self-effacing giant of a man who grew up in nearby Orem, Utah, and who, prior to coming to Provo had never coached a winning team. The same man who has become one of the winningest coaches of all time and who *USA Today* has described as a *national coaching treasure*. We could visualize chapters about the creation and development of the now-fabled quarterback factory which has produced a Heisman trophy winner, a NFL Most Valuable Player, and no less than seven All-America quarterbacks. There would be chapters about often overlooked but equally important defensive All-Americans, one of whom brought the prestigious Outland Trophy to Provo. There would most certainly be a chapter about BYU's improbably march to the 1984 National Championship.

A lot has happened since that first meeting in 1995. BYU's disappointing finish that year, sharing the WAC title but missing out on a bowl berth for the first time in 18 years, dampened enthusiasm for the project. However, all that turned around in 1996 with a remarkable season that began with a win over nationally ranked Texas A&M in the Pigskin Classic and ended a record setting 15 games later with BYU's first ever New Year's Day bowl victory over Kansas State in the Cotton Bowl. That certainly gave the project momentum and provided a fitting exclamation point for the book. Another important factor in making this project a reality was when Steve Cameron left Kansas City in early 1996 and came to Provo as the new Sports Editor of the *Daily Herald*. Not only would this give him firsthand knowledge of the subject matter and a fan's passion for BYU football, but he would also become half of a very experienced and successful team which included longtime *Daily Herald* writer, author and BYU watcher, Dick Harmon. It immediately became clear that combining the talents of both experienced writers would make this a much better book. Another thing became clear. The last important ingredient needed to ensure the success of this narrative and pictorial history of BYU football was a photographer whose talents and reputation are above reproach — whose photographs are already known to many who would purchase the book. In these pages you will enjoy the immense talents of photographer Mark Philbrick who has been the University's official photographer for the past 21 years. Mark has attended virtually every important scrimmage and game during that time and his photographs have won numerous regional and national awards.

And, of course, every great story needs a climax. The snub of BYU by the so-called Bowl Alliance, despite its 14-1 record and fifth place national ranking outraged people all over America and created such a furor that Senate hearings were eventually conducted on the matter. Many who might not have otherwise heard about the BYU Cougars become overnight supporters of this team who epitomized what's good about college athletics. Ironically, it was these same underdog Cougars who just over a decade before had burst into the national spotlight with a perfect 13-0 season and what many consider to be the most controversial National Championship in NCAA Division I history. Few have forgotten the 1984 Cougars and the 1996 Cougars will likely be the same.

Yes, this is a great story, told magnificently through word and picture in these pages. But it is also a story that will most certainly require a sequel. We hope you'll agree.

HALE
25

Introduction

SPECIAL PLACE.

Special team.

Consider this: On a cold, drippy day in May of 1997, perhaps 3,000 hearty souls bundled up for the privilege of spending a morning on a jostling trek around the soggy East Bay golf course in Provo. Dark clouds covered the Wasatch Mountains and the skies to the west over Utah Lake seemed swollen with the prospect of rain.

These folks who chose to ignore or defy the weather forecast weren't on the links to play.

Instead, the paying public turned out to watch a nine-hole event called the Provo Open Skins Game. Four PGA touring pros with Utah ties—Dan Forsman, Mike Reid, Keith Clearwater and Jay Don Blake—were teeing it up in this popular charity event.

But even these pros weren't the main attraction.

No, the crowd was far more interested in their playing partners, each one a former Brigham Young quarterback. With all due respect to the professional golfers, you probably could draw a pretty good audience just to watch Ty Detmer, Jim McMahon, Marc Wilson and Gifford Nielsen in a celebrity oil-changing contest.

In the order in which they were just introduced, the four gunners rank first, second, sixth and eighth on BYU's all-time passing chart; which is to say, they all

"I'VE SAID THIS TO ANYONE WHO WILL LISTEN TO ME: LAVELL IS ONE OF THE TOP FIVE COACHES TO EVER COACH THE GAME OF FOOTBALL."

– GRANT TEAFF, PRESIDENT
AMERICAN FOOTBALL
COACHES ASSOCIATION

deserve to be mentioned with the best collegiate throwers in history, and they are nothing short of icons representing a spectacular program which has become synonymous with offensive excellence over the past quarter-century.

Now, the audience that chilly morning no doubt was too caught up in the fun of the event—not to mention warding off occasional goose-bumps—to think much of who was missing from the festivities. But to put the incredible legacy of BYU football in even clearer perspective, let's call a partial roll of some quarterbacks who skipped the local version of the '97 Skins Game: Robbie Bosco, No. 3 in all-time passing yardage and quarterback of BYU's 1984 national championship team; John Walsh (No. 4), who threw for a 8,390 yards and 66 touchdowns despite time lost to an injury; Steve Young (No. 5), distant relation to the university's namesake, a Super Bowl winner with the 49ers and quite possibly the pro game's best quarter-back in the 1990s; and Steve Sarkisian (No. 7), who wrapped up his two-year stint at BYU with a Cotton Bowl victory on Jan. 1, 1997, after directing the Cougars to a 14–1 record (best ever in Division I-A), and leading the nation in passing.

The aforementioned eight QBs and a handful of other hurlers have thrown for more than 42 miles of yardage since BYU instituted its version of the West Coach offense in 1973, several years before the thing ever caught on with the pros.

"We've been lucky. We've had some guys who could pull the trigger," says LaVell Edwards, the ringmaster who led BYU out of the football wilderness when he was promoted to head coach 25 years ago.

Lucky?

Well, that's LaVell, a unbelievably modest fellow considered so low-key that some worry he might doze off on the sidelines. This is the gentlemen whose expression is consistently dour to the point that the most famous statement ever made about him came from former BYU golf coach Karl Tucker: "LaVell's really happy. He just forgot to tell his face."

Everyone in Utah knows that line by now. Maybe even some folks outside the Mountain Time Zone have heard it in passing. Pun intended. Far fewer, however, truly have grasped the enormous success of BYU football.

Or the staggering odds against which it was accomplished.

Just to touch on the numbers, Edwards is ninth on the Division I-A list of all-time victories with 228 (averaging nine per season), fourth among active coaches behind only Joe Paterno, Bobby Bowden and Tom Osborne. LaVell has won 18 Western Athletic Conference titles in 25 seasons, and his high-octane offense keeps adding to its ongoing record of 275 games without being shut out.

Don't bother with that old gripe

about BYU's relatively soft schedule, either. Just ask Penn State or Miami. Try Michigan, Texas and Oklahoma. They've all lost to BYU. And so has Notre Dame—in South Bend.

Sorry, but there's nothing fluky about the Cougars, who could play in any league, any time.

Edwards?

"I've said this to anyone who will listen to me: LaVell is one of the top five coaches to ever coach the game of football," says Grant Teaff, former Baylor boss and now president of the American Football Coaches Association.

Edwards has been courted by several big-time schools over the years, and once seriously considered an offer from the Detroit Lions. But he's always chosen, in the end, to stay at home. LaVell's legend basically will revolve around just one employer, the Mormon school just up the road from his boyhood home in Orem.

Roots are part of it, of course, and so is that unbreakable bond with the Church of Jesus Christ of Latter Day Saints.

Ironically, the fact that BYU is LDS-owned and operated, that 98 percent of the student body is Mormon and that everyone on campus must sign an Honor Code—requiring abstinance from alcohol, tobacco and harmful drugs in addition to living an honest and chaste existence—makes the Cougars' football saga even more compelling.

When Edwards first arrived on campus as an assistant in 1962, it was generally assumed that the church affiliation, plus large numbers of athletes leaving for two-year LDS missionary stints, pretty much made success a pipedream.

In the 30 years prior to Edwards' ascension to the head coaching job, BYU had exactly eight winning seasons.

And yet this unassuming man not only reversed that trend, he's taken the Cougars to the mountaintop. Now an unquestioned national powerhouse,

BYU plays in a state-of-the-art, 65,000-seat stadium and regularly entertains national TV audiences.

Edwards and his staff have added rock-solid defense to the equation, and in 1996, they actually made their relentless passing game even more dangerous by acquiring the will and the athletes to the run the ball.

By the time BYU whipped Big 12 power Kansas State 19–15 in the '97 Cotton Bowl for its 14th victory and a No. 5 ranking in both major polls, you'd have to say the verdict was in: This is the big time.

BYU's success actually carried all the way to Washington, where a congressional subcommittee began hearings on the business of the so-called Bowl Alliance—that confederation of a few major conferences which basically has taken every big-money bowl game hostage.

The beef concerned the Alliance's snub of the fifth-ranked Cougars. Formally, the question before Congress was what to do about equal opportunity for non-member leagues like the Western Athletic Conference, and whether federal anti-trust laws were being abused.

But in reality, the story was BYU. Excluding the Alliance members and Notre Dame, no one but the Cougars has finished with a top-10 ranking since . . . well, almost since the days of leather helmets.

In fact, former BYU tight end Chad Lewis was called to testify at the subcommittee hearings.

Whatever your vantage point—from a Provo golf course to the halls of Congress—there is no denying that BYU now belongs to college football's elite.

And naturally, that's one of the themes of this book.

Not the only one, however.

The early days of football at the little private school in Provo contain some fascinating stories, as well, and there are anecdotes galore from years when no one in Philadelphia or New York could have found Utah on a map.

Even football junkies are surprised, for instance, to learn that LaVell Edwards once coached the nation's leading rusher.

Hopefully, the pictures and test offered here will rekindle memories for a lot of fans and perhaps stoke the fires for many more. BYU's faithful followers aren't stuck simply in Utah Valley, or even within the borders of the Beehive State.

Cougar partisans stretch from coast to coast, from Europe to the South Pacific and all points in between.

They've enjoyed incredible success these past couple of decades, and been entertained beyond anyone's wildest dreams. And so the authors offer a celebration.

It's been a wonderful ride, this rise of BYU football. So spectacular, in fact, that even LaVell was caught smiling.

And how in the world might you ever top that?

BYU
TEXAS A&M

BYU

77
24
78
86

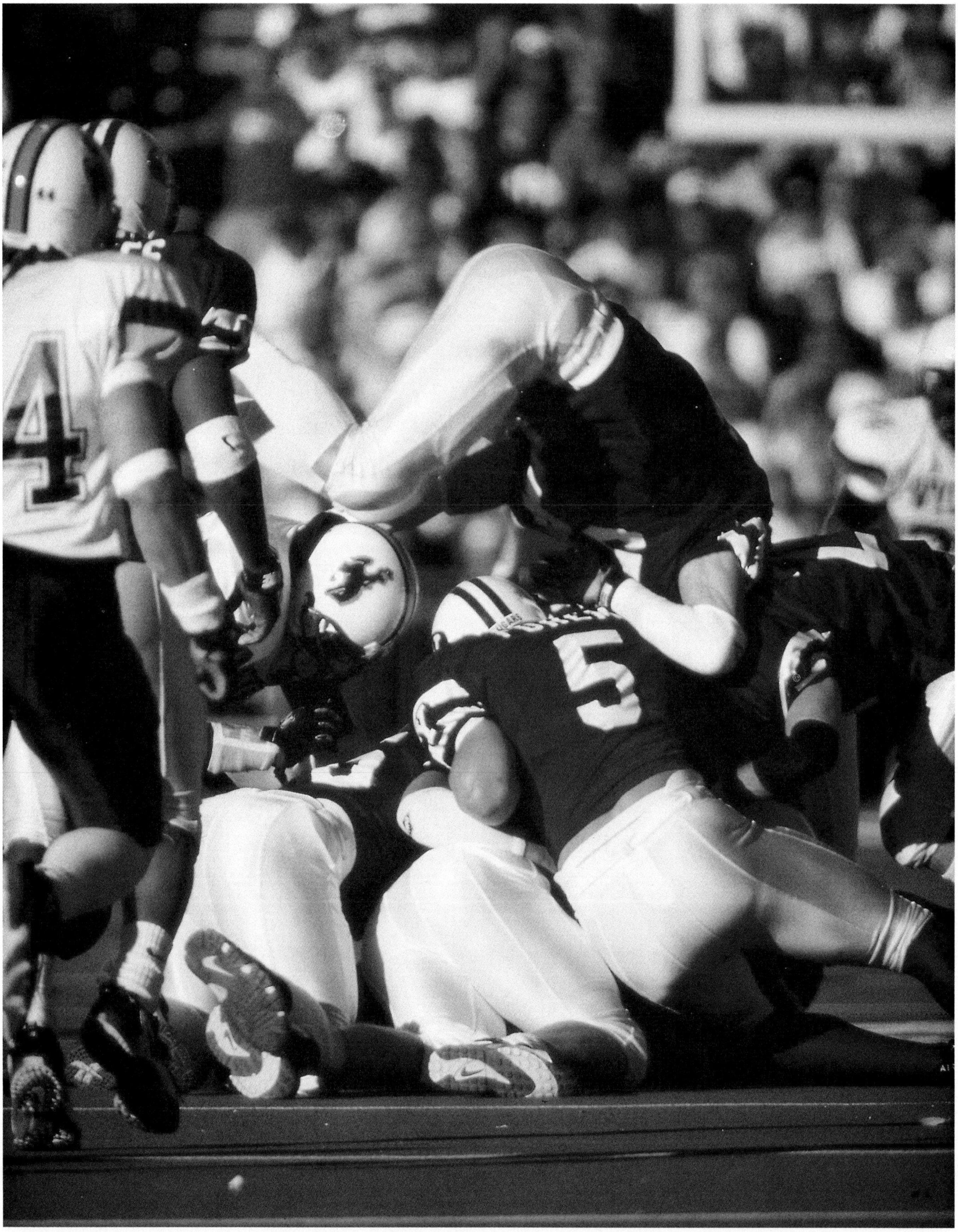

BYU

CHAPTER ONE

LaVell Edwards, athletic director Rondo Fehlberg and all the Cougars celebrate the final seconds of the 1997 Cotton Bowl, BYU's first-ever New Year's Day bowl win.

1

High

"If you don't quit and play hard, I promise you good things will happen."

– LaVell Edwards
BYU Head Coach

Cotton

HANNIBAL used elephants.

Mark Twain used words.

But to get the job done in college football at Brigham Young, you just fling the thing.

And that's exactly what Cougar quarterback Steve Sarkisian found himself doing in Dallas on New Year's Day 1997.

The stage?

The Cotton Bowl, where BYU and its high-flying offense were making their first-ever appearance.

The foe?

Kansas State of the powerful Big 12, also anxious to impress in its first Cotton Bowl date.

Sarkisian and the '96 Cougars overcame an awful lot to play that day. But once again, it was showtime and many doubters across the country were watching.

BYU always has its doubters.

After opening the season with a career passing day that led to a thrilling upset of Texas A&M, Sarkisian shredded plenty of defenses to become BYU's seventh-ranked passer in total yardage. Quite a feat, considering the company and the fact that Sark had played just two seasons as a junior-college transfer.

Quarterback Steve Sarkisian led BYU into the 1997 Cotton Bowl, just as his passes had jump-started the Cougars all season.

Coach LaVell Edwards is known for his stoic demeanor, but the BYU boss got agitated at times during his team's remarkable 15-game season.

Still, what Sarkisian faced in the Cotton Bowl was a national television audience and Kansas State's tough-as-nails defense staring him down. Oh, and most of the college football world was peeking in at this one. There was plenty at stake, including the credibility of a system of choosing a national champion.

Sarkisian, the Cougars, and head coach LaVell Edwards never dreamed back in the hot summer of two-a-day practices that this season would be so long (15 games), so controversial (BYU's snub by the Bowl Alliance), and yet so wonderful.

Edwards, in his 25th season as head coach at BYU, may have turned 66 that fall—a time most men look for a rocking chair—but he was never deeper into a battle plan, his adrenaline pumping, the game as exciting as the first day he hung a whistle around his neck.

Sarkisian?

He'd won the NCAA passing title just like other Cougar quarterbacks of previous years. But in Dallas that day, he faced one of the top secondaries in the country and certainly the biggest test of his college career.

At stake?

A long, seemingly never-ending challenge for BYU. A hurdle, a gauntlet dropped a hundred years ago for the school in laid-back Provo, Utah. BYU must win. Or just look good in losing, so all the critics would somehow see that the Cougars do belong on the field with the big boys.

At BYU, it took half a lifetime to get the sport started after a shaky beginning. The game was even sus-

pended at the old Brigham Young Academy before the turn of the century. Football, the academy's board of directors determined, was too violent.

And it certainly seemed like a lifetime for BYU football to stop being the regional punching bag, not

to mention the annual joke for rival University of Utah.

Once BYU hog-tied the Utes for a respectable stretch, the challenge turned to winning conference championships. Once that was accomplished, the bar was raised higher—a run at building a reputation for success.

And in the lifetime of baby boomers, yuppies, and the current Generation X, BYU's battlefield finally became a national stage.

The Cougars and their followers wanted respect. An element of honor.

"We've never done a better job focusing on the task at hand," Edwards

The famed Cotton Bowl in Dallas was awash in Kansas State purple and BYU blue on New Year's Day 1997.

To win, BYU would need big games from stars like tight end Chad Lewis, who could go airborne for extra yardage.

In what promised to be a tight defensive battle, the Cougars had to get points from senior kicking star Ethan Pochman.

The Cotton Bowl was no walk in the park, as K-State cornerback Chris Canty proved by knocking the ball away from K.O. Kealaluhi.

said of his Cotton Bowl team prior to kickoff. "We've played well. We are comparable with some of my better teams, but I don't like to compare. We've got more speed than we've had in recent years. We've had great unity. And we've handled the length of the season quite well."

For Sarkisian, the battle was the same.

The characters had changed over the years, but the plot line had the same script: BYU must defeat Kansas State to end the season 14–1 and ranked No. 5 in the national polls.

But this time there was an added twist. BYU found itself carrying the load for more than one-third of Division I college football teams, all of whom—by virtue of their conference affiliation—were outcasts from the big-bucks Alliance.

Left out in the cold were teams like BYU from the WAC and other conferences such as the Big West, Conference USA and the Mid-American. The bowl Alliance addressed this problem in its charter, saying two at-large berths would be awarded. One of these, it was understood, was pretty much the property of Notre Dame, a major independent and TV favorite—if the Fighting Irish won at least seven games.

Sarkisian stood on the turf in the Cotton Bowl that New Year's Day because the Alliance's at-large offering had turned into a national shame, drawing criticism from coast to coast.

In the first-ever conference championship game in the expanded Big 12, there was an upset. Texas shocked No. 2-ranked Nebraska. But Nebraska then got an at-large Alliance Bowl berth in the Sugar Bowl. And instead of inviting BYU, the Alliance turned to Penn State, a lesser-ranked member of the Big 10, to play in the Fiesta Bowl against Texas.

Notre Dame didn't qualify—in fact, after losing to Southern California in the season finale, head coach Lou Holtz resigned. Notre Dame's administration decided the Irish would stay home.

BYU was 13–1 and ranked No. 5, but the Alliance decided to keep its money in the family by handing the at-large berths to Nebraska and Penn State, both of whom had lost twice in the regular season.

When bowl invitations were announced, there were a lot of unhappy campers in the Rocky Mountains; specifically, around Provo.

WAC commissioner Karl Benson had hinted early in the season that the league might file an anti-trust suit against the alliance if BYU or Wyoming had a qualifying ranking for an Alliance bowl but was shut out.

Following the snub of BYU, Benson wasted little time voicing his displeasure.

"BYU did all it could. We did all we could," Benson announced. "I said I would be shocked if BYU was not in an Alliance bowl. I am shocked. BYU meets every criteria they want in terms of ranking, tradition, players, a legendary coach, record, fan support and tradition of television ratings."

Benson claimed the snub was a mystery. He then flew to New York City for a meeting with commissioners of the six Alliance conferences and the four conferences that had been left out.

In days, weeks, then months to come, Benson and presidents of WAC schools shot off a round of proposals and counter-proposals which led to congressional hearings and preparation of a lawsuit.

But no proposals could do anything for the 1996 Cougars.

Edwards, typically, tried not to stoke the fire of controversy in days following the announcement of bids.

"We did all we could do in winning 13 games and climbing where we are in the rankings," he said. "But the rest of it is out of our control. When the major conferences were included in the Alliance, they left out the WAC.

"The only way we could get in is through two at-large berths left open. At No. 5, we were not one of those selections. If that doesn't get it done,

LaVell looked grim, but what else was new?

The magic season really started with a phenomenal victory over Texas A&M and its talented quarterback, Branndon Stewart.

BYU moved the ball consistently against A&M, but receivers like Kaipo McGuire had to pay for it.

The opener against A&M marked the start of a breakout season for gifted tight end Itula Mili.

then perhaps a team from our league will never be in if it stands the way it does today."

BYU defensive captain Shay Muirbrook could not hide his disappointment. "It's not fair to have someone else tell you how good you are," he said. "It's tough when you do not get a chance and you cannot let it be determined on the field. The guys making this decision have never been on the field against us."

Those guys making the decision—or at least representatives of the business cartel (bowls, television networks and conferences)—did make an appearance on that CBS bowl announcement show on Dec. 8, 1996.

BYU fans will remember that performance for its hypocrisy.

The network trotted out key Alliance executive directors, coaches of selected teams, and CBS sports analyst Craig James. Edwards received an invitation to be on the program, and reluctantly agreed to a remote interview.

When Fiesta Bowl executive director John Junker explained how previously unranked Texas from the Big 12 would play Big 10 also-ran Penn State with his No. 12 ranking, he tried hard to show how it was a solid sell. Based, he claimed, on competition.

"Our committee saw great parity in the teams ranked No. 5 through 12, and these two teams brought the most plusses to the table," Junker said.

A little embarrassed for his friend Edwards, Penn State coach Joe Paterno almost apologized for BYU not receiving the invitation given to his team.

"What would be better than this is a method of ranking teams that is not political," Paterno said.

James, a former SMU running back, went right ahead and asked the "BYU question" for the panel. James didn't get a straight answer from anyone.

The one person who tried was Orange Bowl president Keith Tribble, but his quote became a joke in Provo as soon as it left his mouth.

Alluding to Nebraska playing unranked Virginia Tech in the Orange Bowl, Tribble said: "What could be better than two teams with 10-win seasons?"

Well, how about two ranked teams, one with a 13-win season?

James finally said, "I look forward to seeing a true playoff system where a national champion is matched up and a team like Brigham Young is not left out of it."

Kramer, the man who put the Alliance together, weakly explained in response to James: "Well, primarily, the object is to put together the best teams to play each other and slow down the selection process so there is time to get the teams truly deserving of a bowl matchup. It is very important to preserve the bowls."

And more importantly, as Kramer didn't bother to add, preserve the money.

When all the chips were counted, the Big 10 earned $22 million by sliding Penn State into an Alliance bowl ahead of fifth-ranked BYU. The Big 12 got $21.37 million, the SEC $14 million and Big East $11 million.

That dramatic victory over Texas A&M came down to K.O. Kealaluhi's touchdown catch in the final minute. K.O. cradled Steve Sarkisian's perfect throw, then found himself being mobbed by joyous teammates.

After two wins to open the 1996 season, the Cougars were outhit and outscored by a tough Washington team in rainy Seattle. Rashaan Shehee (1) scored twice for the Huskies.

The Pac-10, which became an Alliance member in 1997, earned $11.2 million.

Meanwhile, the WAC—snubbed just about as overtly as is possible—earned $2.7 million with just BYU and Utah going to bowl games. The WAC qualified Wyoming, Colorado State, Air Force, and San Diego State for bowl games and had to settle for the barest minimum.

All this talk of money, the Alliance and assorted controversies proved to be important motivational fodder for BYU that day in Dallas. Kansas State might not be the biggest name in college football, but the Wildcats had gone 9–2 and they represented the hated Big 12.

In other words, the Alliance. If K-State whipped the Cougars, Roy Kramer and his pals would be doubled up with laughter.

For BYU, the added incentive in the Cotton Bowl was to show the country that this was a team to be taken seriously.

That campaign actually began the previous year.

In 1995, the Cougars tied for the WAC title, but did not go to a bowl game for the first time in 16 years. That junior-dominated group vowed to earn some respect the following year.

The '95 team had been hindered by internal strife. Some players on both sides of the line pointed fingers at those they believed were the cause of losses.

The bottom came in a game against Utah at Cougar Stadium, in which the Utes humiliated BYU 34–17. Limping with injuries in the secondary, BYU's defense struggled, and the offense fared no better with Sarkisian throwing four interceptions.

But even worse, several BYU players on the sidelines were selfishly throwing tantrums over playing time, even shoving each other.

That loss to Utah was the Cougars' third straight, and it left a cloud over the program. The gloom affected fans, players and coaches. The Cougars had posted a 7–4 record, but it was not BYU football. Following a season-ending win over Fresno State, many fans talked of shaking up BYU's program, even replacing some coaches.

But the team had ideas of its own. The players wanted to re-shape their own attitudes and purge both bad feelings and and a lost season.

"We just had to turn it around," tight end Chad Lewis vowed following the 1995 season. "We want to return BYU to its tradition of winning football. That means winning the conference, making opponents respect us on the field, playing outstanding defense and going to a bowl game."

Lewis joined a group of seniors who committed to themselves to work hard in the off season, through the winter of 1996 and into the spring. When Lewis and his mates showed up for spring practice, Edwards noticed a new attitude.

Coaches can lecture, even yell and scream. Coaches can lay out the X's and O's for players. But chemistry is something that comes from within the squad. The seniors who were determined to rejuvenate BYU took on a mission and an attitude.

It carried over to two-a-day practices in the summer.

"I don't think I've ever had a team that got along so well and actually enjoyed coming out to practice and being together," Edwards said.

Two events inspired everyone.

The first was the appearance of preseason magazines, polls and the vote of the media at the WAC meetings in Las Vegas during July. Utah, which returned the most starters was favored to win the conference. Not only that, media voters suggested, but the Utes had the most talent, the quickest team and even the best coaching staff. One magazine suggested that Cougar middle linebacker Muirbrook was the most overated player in the league.

The second event was BYU athletic director Rondo Fehlberg signing a contract guaranteeing a gate of $1 million for the Cougars to host Texas A&M in the Pigskin Classic on Aug. 25 in Provo.

The game against the Aggies (ranked No. 12 in the preseason polls) would be televised nationally by ABC and kick off the college football season.

This matchup also would challenge the Cougars to start the season earlier than usual—July for incoming freshmen. And it opened the door, with the first ever WAC championship game set for Dec. 7, for a possible 15-game season.

No Division I football program ever had played 15 games. So the goals were out there, and the Cougars were hungry.

For all the recognition Edwards receives for explosive offenses, the veteran coach knows that championships are contructed on great defenses. And special teams.

And sure enough, the building blocks for the Cotton Bowl-bound Cougars began with defense and the kicking game, when BYU's coaching staff turned to junior college transfers and two key young players who had redshirted as freshmen. And a guy with no experience whatsoever.

None of the prognosticators could guess how good BYU's defense might become in 1996 because so much depended upon new faces, combinations that were unproven.

To be a great team—along the lines of 14–1—the Cougars had to get lucky with personnel. For instance, BYU needed a kicker. Their best candidate was Ethan Pochman, a converted soccer player and senior. He'd never kicked a field goal in a real football game in his life.

A gamble?

Obviously, but Pochman shocked everyone but his coach, Chris Pella, in 1996. Pochman epitomized the spirit of the entire season by doing what nobody thought he could. He ended up breaking the school season scoring record with 123 points, made 61 consecutive PATs, (another record) hammered a 51-yard field goal at Tulsa, the fourth best in BYU history.

And to top off his single season BYU career, Pochman kicked the game-tying field goal in the first-ever

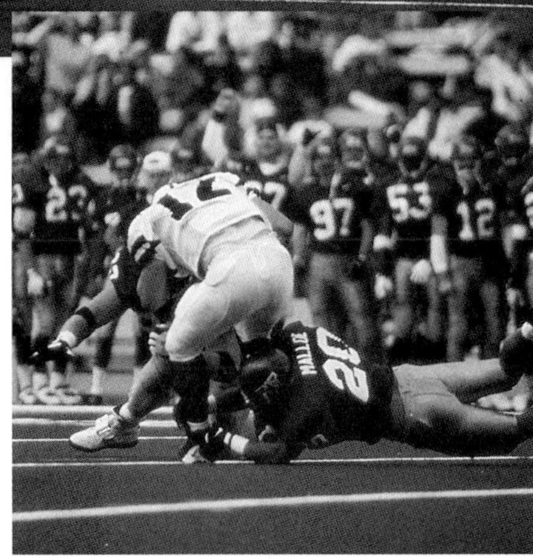

Washington's rugged defense brought the Cougs back to earth, as fullback Dustin Johnson was gang-tackled and QB Steve Sarkisian endured eight sacks.

Leadership was crucial to the '96 Cougars team captains (from left) Shay Muirbrook, Chad Lewis, Tim McTyer and Steve Sarkisian.

WAC championship game against Wyoming, then nailed the overtime winner to give his Cougars their first championship in the "New WAC."

The Cougars got an infusion of quickness when they signed Tim McTyer from Los Angeles Junior College in 1995. McTyer, who played safety and halfback in high school, earned All-America honors in junior college. A hard-hitting tackler, McTyer turned a lot of heads his junior year at BYU. Entering his senior season, McTyer gained 12 pounds and looked tougher than ever at his right cornerback spot.

BYU's secondary had struggled in the early '90s. Working without depth or speed, many BYU championship teams in the Ty Detmer and John Walsh eras had to outscore opponents because opposing quarterbacks could pick on Cougar cover men and do a lot of damage.

The Cougars got very lucky when they signed the nation's top JC cornerback in 1997. Omarr Morgan, nicknamed "The Blanket," was an All-American at El Camino Junior College in southern California.

Morgan got BYU's attention early in the season because the Cougars had mined El Camino for two straight years, including the signing of Sarkisian, who led the nation in passing there his sophomore season in 1994.

When BYU recruiters signed

Morgan's teammates Chris Ellison (safety), and Darin Sagapolu (center) from coach John Featherstone's team, Sarkisian worked hard to convince Morgan he was sorely needed in Provo.

Morgan ended up turning down scholarship offers from Texas A&M and Arizona State to sign with the Cougars. That one move elevated BYU's secondary from below average to the top pass defense in the WAC.

The Cougars had snatched JC defensive tackle Henry Bloomfield from Dixie College the previous season. As a senior, Bloomfield would be the anchor for the interior line. With returning starters Daren Yancey and end Ed Kehl already on board, Edwards was counting on junior Harland Ah You to help shore up the defensive line.

Byron Frisch, a 6-6, 260-pound redshirt freshman, would be getting his first playing time. Frisch broke his ankle in spring practice, but an amazing recovery enabled him to earn a starting spot at defensive end when two-a-days began.

Frisch was BYU's quickest lineman during the shuttle sprints on the first day of fall practice.

The other key young player was sophomore linebacker Brad Martin, who came to BYU out of Fresno's Clovis West High. The thing was, though, Martin had been named the best quarterback in northern California.

Quick, strong and smart, Martin also had been a star in the secondary at Clovis West. BYU coaches thought they recognized a potentially sensational outside linebacker.

In the middle, the Cougars would rely on Muirbrook, a true character and well-known non-conformist. Muirbrook was disgusted with his junior season and vowed he would leave Provo by making a mark for himself.

As the defensive leader for the Cougars, Muirbrook became the most feared player in the 16-team WAC by the end of the season.

However you looked at things prior to the '96 season, though, this was a team—and a defense—with all sorts of question marks to go with the new faces and new attitudes.

The offense turned up some surprises, too.

Sarkisian was expected to produce a lot of numbers when he took over the Cougar attack in 1995 and did so right on cue, but he fell short of filling the shoes of several former BYU quarterbacks. In other words, he didn't win enough.

So Sark had his doubters at the beginning of the '96 season, and proved them all wrong.

He led the nation in passing (which was almost old hat at BYU), but also took charge when it mattered. Sarkisian became the unquestioned trigger man of the offense, and throughout the year, he provided huge plays when BYU needed him most.

Another surprise: The Cougars had the worst running attack in school history in 1995, that 7–4 season. And that didn't help Sarkisian, who became target of pass rushers.

BYU sweated out a furious 17–14 victory over New Mexico in Provo, on a day when the ball and everything else seemed to be up in the air.

Linebacker Shay Muirbrook gave BYU a boost in Logan by returning a fumble for a touchdown in a victory over Utah State.

Ronney Jenkins on the loose.

While working to remedy this situation, Edwards hit gold when he signed the No. 2 junior college rusher in the country, Brian McKenzie from Western Arizona. A big, punishing runner, McKenzie would anchor BYU's backfield.

Just weeks after landing McKenzie, Edwards got word that early recruiting efforts in southern California would pay off. A young high school player named Ronney Jenkins was firm in his commitment to sign with the Cougars.

Jenkins made national headlines at Port Hueneme, Calif., when he ran for 619 yards and seven touchdowns in one game. That 619 total broke the national single-game rushing record.

In addition to having 4.3 speed in the 40-yard dash, Jenkins could long jump more than 24 feet and displayed explosive acceleration. This was a potential star, and it was crucial that when other big-time schools came calling, Jenkins stuck to his guns—and to BYU.

The addition of Jenkins and McKenzie gave the Cougars an unproven — but potentially explosive — weapon offensively. But additional good news for Edwards came in discovering an offensive line to go with the pair of talented backs.

Offensive line coach Roger French entered fall drills hoping nine or 10 linemen would emerge. French likes to make linemen interchangable in case of injuries.

French ultimately switched the 6–4, 300-pound Larry Moore from guard to center because of his athleticism. James Johnson, a 6–6, 295-pound tackle, got moved inside to guard. Matt Cox, a 6–6, 290-pounder, was ticketed to man the other guard spot.

Next came the two tackle positions. Here French found a couple of bookends. The first, sophomore Eric Bateman (6–7, 300) had all the talent to be a superstar, but just hadn't been on the field very much. The other was much-ballyhooed freshman John Tait, who'd just returned from an LDS mission. Tait stood 6–7 and weighed 298 pounds, but like all of the starters, he had a flat belly and he was quick.

Most offensive lines in Division I and even the NFL feature huge men, and many have blubber hanging over their belts. Not this version of the Cougar hogs. These were all guys in shape, men who took pride in their appearance, conditioning, and were former track athletes or basketball players.

BYU's receiving corps consisted of typical Cougars.

They didn't have blazing speed, but they hung on to the ball, ran precise routes and could make plays. Seniors Kaipo McGuire and K.O. Kealaluhi would get the starting nod.

On the other hand, the tight ends were bona fide stars, money in the bank for Edwards. In the 6–6, 240-pound Lewis, the Cougars had a preseason All-American candidate. He would be joined by 6–5, 250-pound Itula Mili, who actually had more natural ability than Lewis. Both were outstanding receivers, adequate blockers, and came with five years of experience running BYU's sophisticated multi-formation offense.

Due to freak injuries and other unpredictable events in their careers, neither Mili nor Lewis had played a full season at the same time as the other.

Mili wound up leading the nation's tight ends in receptions and receiving yards most of the season. He had 46 catches, ranking him No. 1. While Mili ended the year—with a leg injury prior to the WAC title game—ranked No. 12 on the school's all-time receiving chart, Lewis finished No. 18.

The Cougars also featured another important weapon. His name was James Dye.

After leading the nation in punt returns in 1995, Dye returned for his senior year at BYU and proved to be not only one of the most exciting playmakers in school history, but a dangerous part of the Cougar arsenal as a pass-receiver and occasional threat to bust loose on a reverse.

So the stage was set for a Cougar resurgence in 1996.

The will and attitude was outstanding—Edwards hadn't ever seen it better. The talent level was higher than most outsiders realized, and best of all, most of the team's question marks would turn into positives.

But there was still a season to play, and it started with a bang.

Texas A&M.

The Big 12.

On national TV.

The last time the Aggies played BYU was in the 1990 Holiday Bowl, and it was a game Cougar fans would rather forget. Heisman Trophy winner Ty Detmer sufferred two separated shoulders. A&M applied a 65–14 whipping that was a humiliating experience.

After Detmer was injured and lying on the ground with his second separation, Aggie players mimicked him by falling to the ground, kicking their legs in the air in feigned pain.

Aggie coach R.C. Slocum, meantime, had used halfback passes and other trick plays in the fourth quarter to rub it in.

Cougar fans never forgot that day.

Now here was a chance to avenge that disaster in San Diego.

Texas A&M brought its highly publicized "Wrecking Crew" defense to Provo. With exception of the Aggie secondary, most key players from the unit which was in the NCAA's top 10 in '95 were returning.

This figured to pose a big problem for Sarkisian, not to mention his new and inexperienced line and backs.

"Going into the season opener, I thought I had really learned a lot about this offense. But at that point you have no idea how complicated things can get in a game situation," Sarkisian said.

The Pigskin Classic really was—a classic.

It fell on a beautiful summer day in Provo. Temperatures by the mid-morning kickoff were in the mid-80s and eventually soared to the high 90s by halftime.

Since this was the only game of the day, a good share of the curious college football world looked in for a televised preview.

Nobody gave BYU a chance.

Oddsmakers and assorted other guessers nailed the Cougars as big underdogs, anywhere from 17 to 31 points. A&M, after all, was favored to

Back and rumbling: Dustin Johnson rolls for big yardage as the Cougars get jump-started against SMU.

James Dye was a multi-purpose weapon, both on offense and kick returns. When he got free, Dye was always a threat to wind in the end zone and then celebrating in the stands.

challenge for a division championship in the new Big 12 and people in Texas were talking about a possible run at a national title.

The Aggies were counting on Tennessee transfer Branndon Stewart to provide an added dimension on offense—the pass. The 6-foot-5, 235-pound Stewart was a backup to Payton Manning for the Vols, and many thought this native Texan should have beaten out Manning.

Now he'd transferred back to the Lone Star State and the most feared team in the old Southwest Conference.

The script held form early, as the Cougars fell behind 20–6 and Sarkisian struggled to complete drives. But the Aggies played BYU man-on-man defensively and slowly the Cougars were making adjustments.

BYU's offense always has been geared to tear up man-to-man defenses.

So as the clock ticked down towards the fourth quarter, a nationwide audience saw all it wanted of Sarkisian and BYU's presumed pop-gun offense, which shreaded and humiliated Slocum's Wrecking Crew.

The Cougs, in fact, set A&M on a reeling course from which the Aggies never really recovered the rest of the year.

Sarkisian staged a final dramatic comeback, the third such charge in four quarters, tossing a perfect spiral to Kealaluhi, who caught the ball in stride and skidded into the end zone on his back.

The winning 46-yard touchdown pass lifted unheralded BYU to a 41–37 victory over the freshly humbled Aggies.

Just as the upset seemed to knock the life out of A&M, likewise it acted like a booster rocket for respect-starved BYU. Cougar coaches later labeled K.O.'s catch as the biggest play of 1996.

How huge was this win?

A Houston television station reported the week of the game that Big 12 officials were considering an invitation for BYU to join the league.

The win didn't dampen discussion.

And there is no team in the solar system BYU fans wanted to beat more than Slocum's Aggies (not counting Utah, of course).

Kealaluhi, whose parents arrived from Hawaii for the only game they would see on the mainland, watched as the senior from Maui rode the shoulders of teammates off the field, a scene reminiscent of the 1990 season-opening Cougar upset of No. 1 Miami.

Here's how the Aggies went down: With BYU trailing 37–34 and 1:23 to play in the game, Sarkisian was just about out of bullets. He had to deliver.

Sark waltzed the Cougars to the winning score from his own 22-yard line, and he did it in 23 seconds.

Operating from the shotgun, Sarkisian connected with roommate Kaipo McGuire for 11 yards, then hit Kealaluhi for 21 yards and a first down at the A&M 46.

During an injury timeout, BYU had the luxury of drawing up a set play. With the Aggies stubbornly still playing man defense in the secondary, Kealaluhi smoked corner Shun Horn, cutting outside and then steaking downfield along the sideline.

Sarkisian timed his pass perfectly.

"I saw the ball in the air, and wondered if I'd have to make a dive for it," Kealaluhi said. "But Steve led me just right and I caught it in full stride."

Sarkisian said A&M was pressing man-on-man on the line. "And we

Rice was supposed to offer a huge challenge to BYU's WAC title hopes, but running back Brian McKenzie (20) and the Cougs trampled the Owls, 49–0.

Junior Brian McKenzie was a reliable runner, blocker and pass receiver all season.

More defense: Bryon Frisch just won't let Utah quarterback Mike Fouts get away.

took a chance," he said. "You have to take chances."

Sark wound up ripping A&M's famed defense for 536 yards and six touchdown passes. His passing efficiency, with the ghosts of Jim McMahon, Steve Young and Ty Detmer hanging in the air, was a whopping 217.78.

"I've felt good about this team all fall camp, and this was a great effort," Edwards said afterward. "This is a tremendous opening game. I hoped we'd have time to pass. Our offensive line played superb after being a question coming in. Everybody stepped it up."

Sarkisian praised his new offensive line, and suggested that the Cougs' up-front guys simply wore down the Wrecking Crew in the fourth quarter.

BYU drew first blood on a 5-yard touchdown throw from Sarkisian to Lewis, whose one-hander proved key. With Ethan Pochman's point after blocked, and his failure to convert on two others and a field goal later in the game, the missing five points came into play down the stretch.

A&M jumped ahead 20–6 lead on Kyle Bryant field goals of 45 and 43 yards, along with Sirr Parker's 19-yard run.

"We were going three and out, three and out. But we were almost making the plays that would have got first downs," Sarkisian said.

Then BYU got a big break when Aggie returner Michael Jennings couldn't find the handle on Alan Boardman's low-bouncing punt and BYU freshman Greg White pounced on the ball at A&M's 22.

In the press box, BYU vice president R.J. Snow broke out in a loud cheer, an act prohibited in that area. "I guess I'll have to leave the press box," said Snow, smiling.

That turnover changed the game.

On BYU's seventh play, Sarkisian's bootleg play-action pass found Itula Mili open for a 9-yard touchdown.

BYU forced a punt and Sarkisian drove the offense 74 yards in 10 plays, and with 49 seconds left in the half, Sark tied the game on a dart to Kaipo McGuire in the back of the end zone.

A&M took advantage of an interception to score on a 40-yard touchdown by Eric Bernard, but Sarkisian answered with a 51-yard post bomb to McGuire, drawing BYU to 27–26 after Pochman missed the PAT.

The Aggies scored 10 more points and by the fourth quarter, they'd grabbed a 37–26 lead on Bryant's 52-yard field goal.

Sarkisian answered with a 12-yard scoring toss to James Dye, then the game winner to Kealahuhi.

"If I had to vote today, I'd have BYU No. 1," said ESPN's Beano Cook. "Of course they're the only 1–0 team. [But] If Sarkisian wasn't a Heisman Trophy candidate before, he should be now."

A number for stat freaks: With the upset of A&M, BYU boosted its home record over teams from Texas to 18–0. Most of those victories came at the expense of UTEP, but Texas and TCU also made the list—and there was more to come later in 1996.

On the other side, A&M's loss marked the first-ever season-opening setback for Slocum, who had been 7–0.

Sarkisian's six touchdown passes doubled his best effort from the '95 season and was the most ever against an A&M defense. Four other quarterbacks over the years had thrown for four TDs, but none since Texas' Rick McIver in 1983.

During the entire 1995 season, A&M allowed just eight passing touchdowns. And here these lightly regarded upstarts from the no-name WAC had torched the Aggies for six in a single afternoon.

In the press box, a contingent of Texans went from complaining about BYU receivers using illegal picks to blaming A&M's young secondary for making the Cougars look like All-Americans.

But in the end, it was BYU's execution, physical conditioning, and mid-season form that did in the Aggies.

"Our offensive line was the story of the game," running back Mark Atuaia said. "They wore their defensive line down, then pounded them in the fourth quarter. When those guys rested on their knees during timeouts, they were sucking wind hard. They were tired."

The Cougar offense gained an average of 8.2 yards per play. Kealaluhi led all receivers with six catches for 151 yards and the winning touchdown. McGuire had seven receptions catches for 146 yards and two touchdowns. Chad Lewis, who had three touchdowns in '95, caught a spectacular one-hander for a 5-yard touchdown on BYU's first possession. James Dye had a couple of catches for 44 yards. Itula Mili had five and Atuaia four.

BYU wasn't just about offense in 1996, as the Cougars proved when they swarmed over Rice's potent option game.

It was an assault.

While Edwards downplayed any revenge factor in this rematch with the Aggies following the 1990 Holiday Bowl blowout, Atuaia and Mili said they had a feeling the night before the game.

"Somebody brought a tape in of Ty Detmer playing against Pittsburgh Friday night and showed it to us," Atuaia said. "It was inspiring. Itula and I played with Ty and he was a great teammate. We wanted to come out and win one for the old man [Ty] to avenge what happened at that bowl game. This victory was dedicated to Ty."

Omarr Morgan, the junior college cornerback who got his first Division I start, had been recruited heavily by

Steve Sarkisian proved that in addition to putting up big numbers, he could lead BYU to wins at crunch time.

Stadium surely had to wonder about losing to Washington and barely surviving the Lobos in back-to-back games.

If only they could have seen the future . . .

As it turned out, New Mexico came as close any WAC team would play the Cougars until the conference title game in Las Vegas.

BYU ended September with a 4–1 record after smashing Southern Methodist 31–3 in Provo. Sarkisian threw for 375 yards, hitting on an almost unbelievable 80 percent of his passes.

This game began a trend for the Cougars, as the young offensive line clearly was feeling more comfortable together and McKenzie and Jenkins started to get their timing down.

The Cougs also were proving week after week that they were a rock-solid fourth quarter team. They'd exhausted Texas A&M, taken the momentum away from Washington, turned aside rallying New Mexico—all in the final quarter, when conditioning really mattered.

October was just plain fun.

BYU bumped its record to 8–1 by running over Utah State 45–9 in Logan—significant because the Aggies upset WAC favorite Utah in the season opener—bombing lowly UNLV 63–28, unleashing a startling 257-yard rushing attack in a 55–30 win over Tulsa and finally whipping Texas Christian 45–21 in Fort Worth.

By this time, the Cougars had climbed to No. 13 nationally, the spot they occupied before that disaster at Washington. Now talk began about BYU possibly going undefeated the rest of the way and, yes, deserving to play in an Alliance game on New Year's Day.

In the midst of an exhuasting stretch—ten straight weeks without a rest—the Cougars thumped UTEP 40–18 in Provo on Nov. 2, and turned their attention to a stretch run for the WAC title with a showdowns against Rice and Utah.

While BYU was taking care of business against UTEP, Rice absolutely pummelled the Utes that same day, and the Owls' flexbone offense—with nearly 600 yards rushing—left Utah looking like a high school team.

Rice's visit to Provo had nerves on edge, but BYU had a different defensive scheme ready for the flexbone.

The Cougar staff decided to attack Rice defensely (rather than play read-and-react), then run the football as much as possible to keep the Owl offense on the sideline.

It was easy. Almost laughably so.

BYU won 49–0, limiting Rice to just eight first downs and 179 rushing yards. The Owls did not complete a pass. Meanwhile, the Cougars scored 21 points in the second and third quarters to turn this supposed war into a rout.

With Rice dispatched, the Cougars were settled into a pretty clear spot atop the WAC's Mountain Division. But they still needed to win out, which meant no stumbles on a trip to Hawaii and then victory at Utah—against a rival that had beaten BYU three straight times.

The schedule truly favored the Utes.

While Utah got a week off to

prepare for the division battle with BYU on Nov. 23 in Salt Lake City, the Cougars took off on the long trek to Honolulu.

The Cougars arrived in Hawaii during a record storm that even had President Bill Clinton on the run throughout the islands.

But for BYU in '96, weather was just a hurdle to be cleared.

Defensive tackle Henry Bloomfield returned a fumble for a touchdown and Pochman became BYU's single season and career scoring leader by kicking six PATs and a 25-yard field goal in a 45–14 win that was as bizarre as it was predictable.

Hawaii quarterback Glen Freitas actually jumped into the stands to fight some Rainbow fans late in the game.

By that time, the Cougs already were thinking about Utah—and how little time they'd have to prepare. The BYU traveling party got back to Provo on Sunday after flying all night.

Weary but determined, they had no chance to sit back and savor a No. 8 ranking. Edwards braced his team for coach Ron McBride's Utes, who had scored 34 points in each of their last three games against BYU.

That number, plus the three consecutive defeats to the guys just up the road, stuck in everyone's craw.

It showed.

The Cougars utterly overwhelmed Utah 37–17, clinching the division title and hushing up everyone who had suggested that the Utes were now the state's dominant team.

After playing the Utes three straight times with almost no running attack to help quarterbacks John Walsh and Sarkisian, Cougar coaches this time had the luxury of cramming the ball down Utah's throat at will.

Sarkisian wound up throwing the ball just 12 times, completing a career-low seven, but who cared?

McKenzie rambled for 176 yards and Jenkins had 161 as the Cougars blew the Utes off the line of scrimmage. Even the 20-point margin didn't indicate what a thorough beating the Cougs administered.

At one point late in the game,

The sign said it all as Omarr Morgan and his teammates celebrated their trouncing of the Utes.

Steve Sarkisian seemed ready to take charge as BYU faced off against Wyoming in the WAC's first-ever championship game in Las Vegas.

Linebacker Shay Muirbrook led the way as the BYU shut out Wyoming in the first half.

McBride turned to a sideline TV reporter and said, "They're just tougher than we are."

BYU gained an almost astonishing 376 yards on the ground and held the ball for nearly 38 minutes. It was macho stuff, smash-mouth football—and perfect payback for three straight nightmares.

Any other year, the blowout of Utah would have wrapped up another WAC championship. But not in 1996. What the Cougars earned was a crack at once-beaten Wyoming for the outright conference title.

At the time, it seemed that if BYU beat the Cowboys to finish the regular season 13–1, surely they'd have left the Alliance no choice but to invite some gate-crashers.

But Wyoming wasn't going to be any picnic.

Edwards gave his guys the week off before starting preparations for the Cowboys, a team that had ridden Josh Wallwork's passing and a tough defense to national prominance.

The BYU-Wyoming showdown in Las Vegas turned out to be a gem.

Both teams were ranked, and between them they'd gone 23–2. The attraction wasn't lost on fans, either, as about 20,000 Cougar boosters helped fill 32,000-seat Sam Boyd Stadium and the game drew the best TV ratings of the three conference championships telecast that day.

Poor Wyoming.

In such a setting, you had to feel for Cowboy fans. Not only was Wyoming playing its most heated rival and doing so as an underdog, but other WAC schools wanted the Cowboys to lose so BYU could crack the Alliance—and bring home a huge paycheck.

Not only that, but the Cowboys came into the game knowing coach Joe Tiller was leaving for Purdue. And to top it off, if Wyoming lost—even as Pacific Division champ—the bowl picture looked bleak.

Once hostilities began, BYU got hit hard and quickly.

On his first reception of the game, Mili went down with a season-ending injury, blowing out both sides of his right knee when a Wyoming tackler caught his foot as it stuck to the stadium rug.

Nonetheless, the Cougars took a 13–0 halftime lead, which looked fine—except that BYU stubbornly had continued to run the ball as it had against Utah.

Coug fans who were expecting an offensive show moaned about that first half, and not just because BYU only scored 13 points. Wyoming's pass rush and secondary both were considered suspect, perhaps easy meat for Sarkisian and Co., but the Cowboy air defense hadn't been tested.

And the game was still perilously close.

This time at least, the fans seemed to be right when Wyoming took heart from the modest halftime deficit and began breathing fire. The Pokes completely stuffed BYU's running game in the third quarter—and still there wasn't much throwing—and ultimately scored 17 unanswered points.

Momentum had switched sides, and

the Cougars' dream season—not to mention that possible New Year's Day bowl bid—appeared to be in very deep peril.

Omarr Morgan, the opportunistic cornerback who later saved the Cotton Bowl, probably kept BYU from falling off the edge in the WAC title game, as well.

Wyoming was gearing up for yet another drive with that 17–13, fourth-quarter lead when Morgan stepped in front of a Wallwork pass, handing BYU the ball at the Cowboy 44-yard line.

The Cougs now sensed all kinds of urgency and the passing game was back. Sarkisian hit Lewis for a 13-yard score, regaining the lead at 20–17.

But Wyoming wouldn't die. The Pokes zoomed 80 yards in four plays themselves, then tacked on a two-point conversion that made it 25–20 with 9:24 still to play.

Sarkisian got the Cougs in business again, but this time BYU ran into problems. The passing game was wide open in the middle of the field, but BYU found things jammed up near the end zone and eventually turned the ball over on downs at the Wyoming 2-yard line.

Suddenly the conference championship hung in the balance.

Remember, BYU had been a fourth-quarter team all season, and now the Cougars faced a five-point deficit with the clock winding down and ball in Wyoming's hands.

The BYU defense held, immediately.

The Pokes couldn't move from the shadow of their own goal posts and faced a fourth-and-seven from the 5 with 2:05 remaining.

A punt almost certainly would have given BYU great field position, especially with the dangerous James Dye lurking back near midfield. Still, the Cougs needed a touchdown, and they'd stalled on the previous drive.

Down and out: Healthy most of the year, BYU suffered another key injury in the title game when tight end Itula Mili went down.

Wyoming's Tiller considered his options and picked an odd one.

Tiller chose to take an intentional safety, which allowed the Pokes a free kick from their own 20 but also pulled BYU within a field goal at 25–22 with 1:56 left.

The decision came back to haunt Wyoming.

As expected, the Cougars got the ball in great shape at their own 40 and—considering that the Cowboy defense now was exhausted—Sarkisian found easy targets everywhere.

But BYU still couldn't get further than the Wyoming 3-yard line, at least not in the hurry-up mode, so Pochman was forced to come on and convert a "routine" 20-yard field as the clock expired.

Even though the kick was easy—"It was a PAT, basically," Pochman said—there was plenty of controversy about whether the Cougars should have been allowed to try it.

On that final drive, Sarkisian scrambled for 12 yards to keep things going, but eventually things stalled at the Wyoming 7-yard line with 12 seconds to play.

Defensive lineman Henry Bloomfield makes the play of the championship game, sacking Cowboy quarterback Josh Wallwork in overtime.

Wyoming battled back and forced overtime, threatening to ruin BYU's great season.

Sarkisian was flushed and had to scramble on the next play, and he finally heaved the ball to Atuaia, who made a diving catch inbounds at the 3.

With the clock running.

In fact, the Wyoming bench erupted in celebration, thinking the game was over. There was chaos on the field, until at last the officials ruled that BYU's Kaipo McGuire had called time out with one second remaining.

McGuire claimed he actually began trying to get time called with four seconds on the clock, but that it took the closest official three precious ticks to hear him.

"Yelling is an understatement," McGuire said of his frantic pleas. "I was screaming at the official and doing the timeout sign in front of his face, but he didn't see or hear me for a couple of seconds. Thank goodness, he finally did."

And Pochman delivered.

The overtime format adopted by the WAC was an alternate-possession scenario that has been used for several years in Division I-AA. Each team takes the ball at the opponent's 25 with four plays to make a first down, score a touchdown or kick a field goal.

Obviously, getting the last crack is a huge benefit. BYU won the coin toss and forced Wyoming to give it a shot. No matter what happened, the Cougars—once they got the ball—would know exactly how many points they needed to win or tie.

As it turned out, the Cowboys were cooked. They not only couldn't move the ball forward, but Henry Bloomfield's big sack of Wallwork forced a 47-yard field goal attempt that never had a chance.

So BYU only had to score, any way at all, to close things out.

Edwards took no chances on a turnover or any other crazy sort of thing, and let Pochman decide the WAC championship with a 32-yard field goal.

No problem.

The Cougars' surprise kicking star calmly drilled his fourth of the day, and second under withering pressure, to hand BYU a 28–25 victory, another conference title and that magic 13–1 record.

"It can't get any more exciting than that," gushed the usually stoic Edwards as Cougar partisans stormed

Champions! Ethan Pochman knocks home the winning field goal in OT to give the Cougars a spine-tingling 28–25 triumph over Wyoming.

the field. Edwards even lost his ballcap in the happy crush.

It was fantastic for BYU. And the WAC.

So . . . would the Alliance come calling?

The answer was no.

The killer was Texas' shocking upet of Nebraska on the same day that BYU defeated Wyoming. With previously unranked Texas getting the Big 12's automatic Alliance spot, a bowl home had to be found for Nebraska.

Once the decision came down, Cougar fans groused, and eventually BYU accepted its bid to play Kansas State in the Cotton Bowl.

Interestingly, this was a situation where everyone involved was hungry for respect.

BYU, for all the obvious reasons. Kansas State, as a relative newcomer to higher echelons of college football, never had played on New Year's Day. And the Cotton Bowl, a victim of politics as well, was ommitted from the Alliance and thus hungry to put on a great show.

The Cougar staff refused to let anyone sound unhappy with the trip to Dallas.

For one thing, there was still tons of prestige involved. After all that griping by the WAC, everyone could be pretty embarrassed if the Cougars laid an egg.

K-State was no Little Sisters of the Poor, either, having gone three years without losing to anyone but Nebraska or Colorado.

"We were all about business," Cougar offensive coordinator Norm Chow said. "Nothing became more important than the bowl game."

Chow himself was tested, however. He was named national assistant coach of the year, with ceremonies in Atlanta,

By Cotton Bowl time, BYU was missing some of its firepower. K.O. Kealaluhi (3) was ready to go, but Itula Mili had to watch on crutches.

and promptly was courted for job interviews by Fresno State, California and Arkansas. And sadly, Chow's father died in Hawaii while BYU was in Dallas preparing for the Cotton Bowl.

Meanwhile, Edwards and Kansas State coach Bill Snyder had coached more than 60 years between them, but had never worked sidelines opposite each other.

There was prestige at stake there, too.

In KSU, the Cougars would face the best defense since Washington. The Wildcat secondary featured two-time consensus All-America cornerback Chris Canty. A 5-10, 190 pounder, Canty ran a 4.42 in the 40 and probably would be the best pass defender the Cougars had seen in years.

At a pre-bowl press conference, Canty told the media, "I believe I can cover anybody in the country for three or four seconds."

BYU's Kealaluhi basically agreed and said: "I'll have to be lucky. I'm not the fastest guy in the world in man coverage, but Kaipo and I just have to get off the line and get open."

Canty, Kaipo, K.O., Sarkisian and BYU's own cover guys—Morgan and McTyer—turned out to be pivotal players in the Cotton Bowl, but not always in the way people expected.

Since K-State had run WAC teams Wyoming and Air Force out of the stadium in recent bowl matchups, the Wildcats may have been a little cocky coming to Dallas that week.

They certainly had support, as a record 40,000 purple-clad fans followed the team to Texas. In the days preceding the Cotton Bowl, the place was awash in purple and sometimes it seemed that BYU supporters were hard to find.

The Cougars, meanwhile, continued to act as though this were simply a very important business trip.

At kickoff, the K-Staters were going crazy. But in the end, emotion finally flowed from the Cougars.

BYU was good as Fort Knox gold with everything on the line, rallying for that 14th victory—most in NCAA history—with a thrilling 19–15 triumph that wasn't decided until the final seconds.

This was no Texas shootout, as both defenses ruled the day.

BYU, in fact, could have had a shutout—but for two fluke touchdowns that, until the last two minutes, represented Kansas State's entire offensive production.

The Cats got a score on a deflected "Hail Mary" heave just before halftime and scored in the third quarter as a missed tackle allowed Kevin Lockett to turn a short pass completion into a long touchdown.

When K-State did mount a last-minute drive, Morgan snuffed it out with a clutch interception at the BYU 3-yard line.

When it was over, Edwards was happy, sure. But he also seemed amazed by a team that had begun practice in July, endured an embarrassing loss at Washington and then won

Shay Muirbrook, of all people, opened the bowl game scoring by sacking Kansas State QB Brian Kavanaugh for a safety.

12 straight—including the last two in heart-stopping fashion.

"These guys hung together through 15 games and played hard every week," Edwards said. "This is a marvelous tribute to the kids. We hung in there and kept playing. It's been a special feeling all year long."

Special, yes.

And now there was no question that the Cougars were very, very good.

In the Cotton Bowl, BYU had to be good enough to overcome back-to-back "no-call" pass interference fouls while fighting from behind in the second half.

The missed calls on Ronney Jenkins and K.O. Kealaluhi were so obvious that even the placid Edwards barged onto the playing field. A couple of his assistants nearly went ballistic.

"We won the game, so I guess it doesn't matter," Jenkins said later, "but I'll never understand those two plays. On the sideline, we were thinking that the officials had decided we weren't supposed to win."

BYU also had to be good enough to rally in the fourth quarter—yes, that again—against a bruising defensive unit. But Sarkisian came up with the throws he needed down the stretch, including the game-winner to Kealaluhi.

This victory involved both brains and brawn.

The Cougars scored first on an alert play by Muirbrook, who read a K-State shovel pass in the Wildcat end zone. When defensive end Darren Yancy flattened halfback Mike Lawrence, Muirbrook peeled off and

Tim McTyer (above) heads up field after an interception in the first half of the Cotton Bowl.

sacked quarterback Brian Kavanaugh for a safety.

Converting on Pochman's second field goal try, BYU led 5–0 with just seconds left before halftime. The way both defenses were playing, it seemed touchdowns were out of the question.

Then K-State struck on Kavanaugh's desperation tipped pass as the first half expired. Andre Anderson one-handed the ball off his face mask for a Wildcat touchdown and an 8–5 lead following a two-point conversion.

At halftime, Edwards repeated his 1996 speech for the 15th time: "If you don't quit and play hard, I promise you good things will happen."

After the break, KSU scored again on another weird play, when safety Chris Ellison failed to wrap up Lockett and accidentally bumped him away from the trailing McTyer. Lockett promptly turned a quick slant into a 72-yard TD that put the Wildcats up 15–5.

"Even then, when we were down, I knew we would come back and win," BYU captain Chad Lewis insisted.

Indeed, the Cougars were making inroads even before they scored the critical points. They wore down KSU's defense by controlling the ball for 12 minutes in the third quarter.

In the 70-degree heat—warmest ever for a Cotton Bowl—the Cats began to wilt. Both cornerbacks, Canty and Joe Gordon, suffered dehydration and cramps.

"Our defense was on the field way too long," Snyder said. "We just got awfully tired out there."

BYU had outscored opponents 128–57 in the fourth quarter during the regular season, and the Cotton Bowl was just more of the same.

"The big thing was who could persevere the longest," Edwards said. "I told the guys if we were in it in the fourth quarter, we'd have a shot."

KSU's first fatigue victim was Gordon. Then his heralded cover mate Canty cramped up. And each time Canty went to sidelines, BYU scored on one of the Wildcat backups.

Alert receivers Dye and Kealaluhi burned reserve cornerbacks Demetric Denmark and LaMar Chapman, the latter a freshman with limited playing time, for fourth-quarter touchdowns.

The Cougs started their rally when Dye beat Denmark downfield and hauled in a perfectly lofted 32-yard Sarkisian bomb at the KSU 2, muscling into the end zone with Denmark frantically grabbing at his shoulder pads.

BYU's defense stopped two consecutive Wildcat drives as the clock ticked down to 4:49 and the Cougars, still trailing 15–12, regained possession at their own 40.

Then K-State unintentionally lit a fuse and the Cougars exploded with rage, setting the stage for the first 10-point comeback in a Cotton Bowl win since Texas rallied to whip Alabama 14–12 in 1982.

Trailing K-State in the fourth quarter, the Cougs took inspiration from a vicious hit on a dazed Kaipo McGuire, which was followed by plenty of taunts from the Wildcats.

As the Cougars began to drive, the 170-pound McGuire got his hands on a short pass, turned and was brtually bowled over by safety Mario Smith, who knocked off McGuire's helmet and left him utterly dazed.

Smith started celebrating the big hit. On the KSU sideline, the cramping Canty made fun of McGuire, yelling, "They don't hit like that in the WAC."

Other K-State players laughed at the prone McGuire.

"That was uncalled for," Kealaluhi said. "Kaipo is the smallest man on the field and playing as hard as anyone. They hit was good; making fun of him wasn't."

"It was classless and it made us sick," linebacker Brad Martin said. "They saw us as a peon team from the WAC."

On the next play after Smith's hammer shot, from the K-State 28, Sarkisian took a snap out of the shotgun and looked over at Kealaluhi, who was covered by the freshman Chapman.

"Canty and Gordon had played me bump-and-run just one yard off," Kealaluhi said. "This guy was three yards off and he looked tense and uncertain. We had to go at him."

Kealaluhi exploded downfield, making an inside-out move that Chapman bit on.

Seconds later, the unsung Cougar hero whose game-winning bomb against Texas A&M started BYU's string of 14 wins, hauled in the game-winning pass four yards deep in the end zone.

With Pochman's PAT, BYU led 19–15 with 3:39 to play.

Still incensed about the language directed at his roommate, McGuire, Sarkisian immediately raced over to the KSU sideline and lambasted Canty, drawing an unsportsmanlike penalty on the ensuing kickoff.

When Kansas State mounted one of its classic late-game drives—zooming from its own 28-yard line to the BYU 12 in 13 plays—Morgan killed the Wildcats with that game-ending interception at the 3.

Above: Tight end Chad Lewis made several big catches as the Cougars fought back from a 15-5 deficit.

Top: Muirbrook and the Cougars bottled up K-State all afternoon in Dallas, allowing touchdowns on only two fluke plays.

Payback: One play after K-State knocked out Kaipo McGuire, his Hawaiian buddy K.O. Kealaluhi caught the go-ahead touchdown pass from Steve Sarkisian.

It took huge plays for the Cougars to stave off a furious K-State drive in the final minute. Tim Tyer (21) (inset) knocked All-American receiver Kevin Lockett just over the back line of the end zone to prevent a touchdown, then Omarr Morgan stepped in front of Jimmy Dean (22) for a juggling interception at the 3-yard line to clinch the victory.

There were brains involved in the clinching pick, too. Defensive lineman Ed Kehl heard Kavanaugh call an audible and remembered it from earlier in the game.

Kehl turned to Morgan and hollered, "Slant! Slant!"

Omarr was listening and took care of the rest by stepping inside receiver Jimmy Dean, tipping the ball into the air and cradling it to his chest.

Just prior to Morgan's interception, McTyer made a crucial play of his own when he shoved Lockett just over the back line of the end zone to nullify a possible touchdown.

Muirbrook, meanwhile, was all over the place from start to finish—four sacks, nine tackles and a safety, defensive MVP honors.

"This is probably the best defense we've ever had at BYU," Edwards said. And then, grabbing Muirbrook, he added, "I love the way this guy plays."

Sarkisian tied Roger Staubach's 1964 Cotton Bowl record for completions with 21. The co-offensive MVP (with K-State' Lockett) also came one yard and one attempt from tying two other Cotton Bowl records.

Completing 21 of 36 passes for 291 yards and two touchdowns, Sarkisian finished his Cougar career with a flourish. The former junior-college transfer from California was sacked seven times and knocked down on several more plays.

But when a reporter asked if it was hard to find his wind down the stretch, Sarkisian replied: "Not when they

weren't scoring. "Our defense won this game for us. We were struggling and struggling and somehow pulled it out."

The Cougars outgained KSU 350 yards to 274 and had 24 first downs to

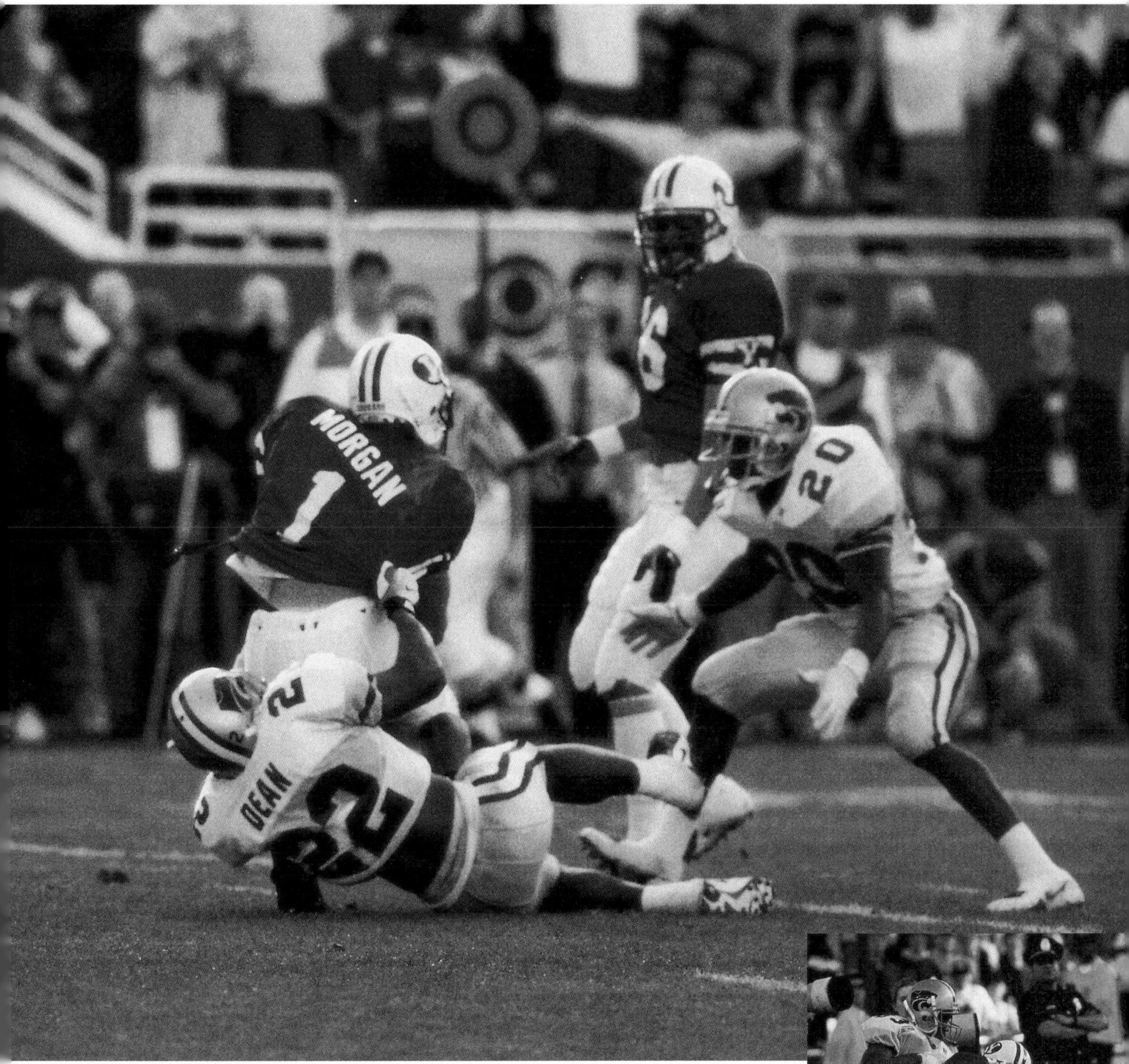

K-State's 14, while holding the ball for seven more minutes. As Snyder suggested, ball control probably decided the game.

Conditioning. Fourth-quarter intensity. The will to win.

"This is awesome, just awesome," Lewis said. "What else can I say?"

Lewis was talking about the Cotton Bowl victory, but he might have meant the entire season.

By any standard, it was awesome.

Cougars

CHAPTER TWO

LaVell Edwards and the troops celebrate their 11-0 regular season and the ascent to No. 1 in the polls in 1984.

2

Champions

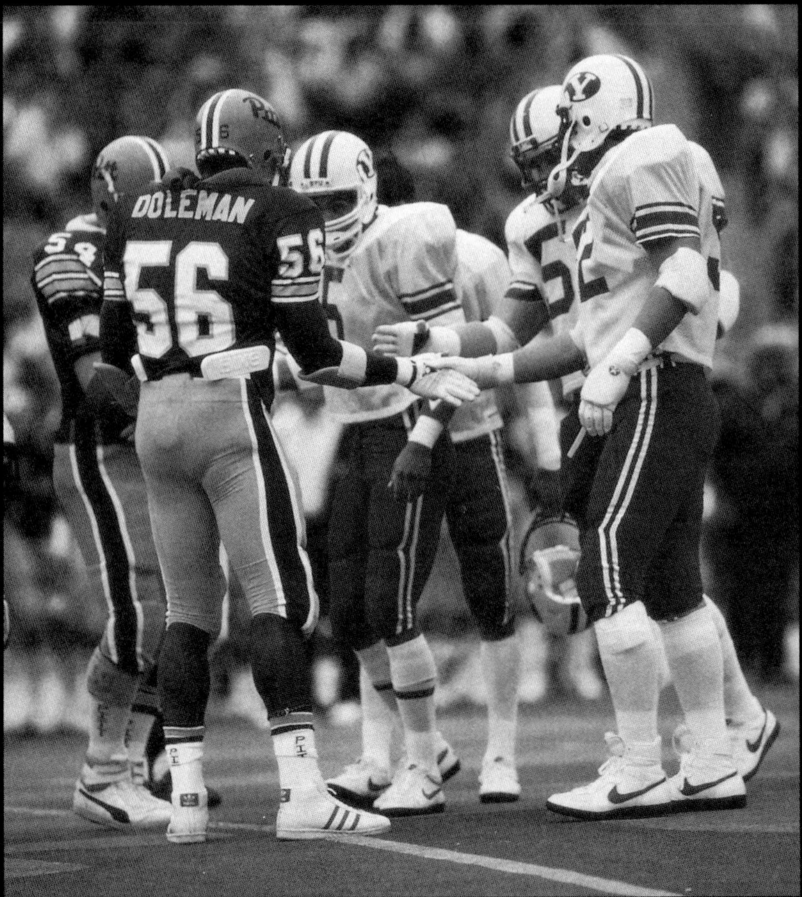

"Sounds like a number one team to me. Sounds like a team Grantland Rice would have scrolled a poem about."

—Jim Murray
Sportswriter

from Nowhere

ROBBIE BOSCO stands atop a tee box, readies his stance, checks his grip, looks down the fairway and begins his backswing.

The golf ball explodes off Bosco's driver, cutting the air in a picture-book draw, then landing and rolling on the grass some 300 yards towards the kidney-shaped green.

His hairline is a little higher these days. There are a few wrinkles at the edges of his eyes. But in very healthy flesh and blood, Bosco remains a symbolic reminder of how an unranked team from nowhere won the mythical national college football championship on heart, guts, and unwavering faith.

Coin toss: Who could have guessed when BYU opened the 1984 season on the road against No. 3-ranked Pitt that the Cougars would be starting their most historic journey?

Bosco is now an assistant coach at BYU. He has a nice home, a beautiful wife, kids, neighbors in suburban Provo. He attends parent-teacher meetings at school, pays taxes and has his cars inspected every year.

He can also whack a golf ball.

Now this may sound like the life of an ordinary Joe, but once upon a time Bosco earned legendary status by limping back onto the turf during the Holiday Bowl at Jack Murphy Stadium in San Diego and leading BYU to its 23rd straight victory and an undefeated season in 1984.

In other words, you can't see Bosco on the golf course or anywhere else around Utah without thinking of those miracle Cougars—perhaps the most improbable

Above: BYU's defense made a statement in front of the national TV audience at Pitt, as Leon White (41) and his mates made life tough for the Panthers.

Top: Robbie Bosco (6) and the BYU offense wasn't exactly a jauggernaut at Pitt, but the Cougars were a resourceful group.

national champs of all time.

That memorable Holiday Bowl and BYU's thrilling 24–17 victory over Michigan sparked a debate that has raged for two decades and someday may lead to a playoff system to determine a college title.

Heaven knows, the idea has been bandied about, hashed and rehashed. Credit those 1984 Cougars for setting the issue on fire.

If it wasn't a columnist somewhere criticizing BYU's No. 1 status heading into the bowl season at the end of 1984, it was NBC's Bryant Gumbel, who uttered the now famous words: "Who have they played? Bo-Diddley Tech?"

And if it wasn't Gumbel, it was that grumbling from Oklahoma's Barry Switzer, who thought his team had played a tougher schedule and deserved more respect. Washington's Don James echoed the same sentiments.

But although many questioned BYU's depth and its schedule, and argued about whether the Cougars were No. 1, the voters in both major polls leaned BYU's way in the end.

The reason?

The Cougars had 12 teams on their schedule, plus a bowl game. They lined up and won every one. In 1984, no other team could make that case.

Vai Sikahema (23) and the rest of the Cougars celebrated their huge victory at Pitt, but they couldn't have known how far it would lead.

BYU fans left no doubt what they thought of broadcaster Bryant Gumbel, who had sneered at the Cougars' schedule and first suggested that they were playing "Bo Diddley Tech."

Jim Murray, legendary sportswriter for the *Los Angeles Times* put it this way: "Sounds like a number one team to me. Sounds like a team Grantland Rice would have scrolled a poem about."

"BYU does a tremendous job," former SMU coach Ron Meyer said during the heat of the No. 1 debate. "And they're a legitimate No. 1—that's all. What else does a team have to do? They throw it, they can play defense, they can put the ball in the end zone against anybody.

"They've got a chance to beat you. With the type of skills they've got, they have a chance to score a lot of points against you."

Then Baylor coach Grant Teaff agreed when asked to compare Oklahoma and BYU, teams ranked first and second heading into the final week of the regular season.

"We played both of them, lucky me, and I think BYU is better," Teaff said. "We felt we had a chance against Oklahoma, but against BYU, all I wanted to do was get the game over with and get out of there."

Support also came from Houston coach Bill Yeoman following BYU's win over Michigan in San Diego: "You win 23 practices in a row nowadays, much less 23 games in a row, and you've really accomplished something."

The Cougars certainly weren't lacking in talent. No less than 15 players from that '84 team were drafted into the NFL, and many of them became stars—including linebacker Kurt Gouveia, return specialist Vai Sikahema, and punter Lee Johnson.

Center Trevor Matich, wide receiver Glen Kozlowski and linebacker Leon White also had pro careers.

Bosco might have had a noteworthy pro career, too, as a third-round draft choice in 1986. But an arm injury

Native San Diegan Leon White soared in the middle of the BYU defense.

The Cougars had their moments on offense, springing Lakei Heimuli into the open.

Robbie Bosco arrived in San Diego a picture of health, but he didn't stay that way.

ruined his chances in the NFL before he really ever got started.

Ironically, that championship team that caused all the national fuss opened the year with huge question marks—especially on offense with the departure of a pair of All-Americans, quarterback Steve Young and tight end Gordon Hudson.

Bosco, a fourth-year junior, was pencilled in to replace Young, but nobody knew how the native of Roseville, Calif., would handle the role.

"Truthfully, I was pretty nervous about it myself," Bosco said. "I think quarterbacks are supposed to be a little bit nervous all the time anyway, but when we opened that season on national TV at Pitt, I was so wound up that I was throwing passes halfway to the moon."

With all of BYU's scoring history, though, the '84 team definitely was built on defense—the finest unit in school history, at least until the 1996 group came along to put up an argument.

BYU did not have exceptional quickness on defense in 1984, but few college defenses ever worked in more harmony than that one. It was as if every player on that side of the ball had a computer chip embedded in his brain and the software that ran it tied every position together in perfect unison.

It sounds corny but the '84 Cougars were friends.

Many of those relationships have continued on, through spouses, children and social circles in business and church. Football office secretary Roselynn Daley once said, "Perhaps that's why they never lost a game. They never lost each other."

Tight end David Mills told reporters at the end of the season that he remembered his teammates as total equals rooting for each other every day.

"A lot of our success is due to the fact that we have no real superstars on this team, and no egos. Each guy has his role and concentrates on doing the job in his assigned role. That's helped us stay real even emotionally all season long."

Athletic director Glen Tuckett concurred, and said: "The team's dedication and cohesiveness was readily observable. No task was too demanding, no adversity was too insurmountable. They snatched victory from impending defeat on more than one occasion."

In fact, the champs came from behind to win four times in 13 games.

It was a team with many heroes, quite a few stars and a ton of role players. But for BYU fans, there are four mental pictures of that group that never will fade away.

The first was a catch by Adam Haysbert, a winning touchdown reception on third down from Robbie Bosco at Pittsburgh.

In the jittery opener. In ESPN's first-ever college football telecast.

The second vision is of receiver Glen Kozlowski dragging himself off the field after a big play, limping and grimacing in pain as if his career might be over—only to race back into the huddle seconds later.

Third picture: That game-winning goal-line stand at Hawaii, when free safety Kyle Morrell made a perfectly-timed dive over the Rainbow center and grabbed quarterback Raphael Cherry's shoulder pads behind his neck while Morrell was completing a full flip.

And the final memory would be of Bosco, his knee banged up so badly he left the stadium on crutches, limping around in the fourth quarter of the Holiday Bowl, leading the Cougars to win No. 13 and the national championship.

Coach LaVell Edwards and his staff, who were both experienced and determined, always have espoused a philosophy that the passing game was the great equalizer, but defense wins championships.

In 1984, both those pieces fell into place.

Veteran BYU assistant coach Dick Felt saw success on the horizon early that year—during spring drills leading up to the perfect season.

"You hate to compare one year to another and say any team is the best," Felt said, "but this team played better and more consistently than any team in a long time. The defensive teams we've had have all been better than they've been given credit for.

"But right from the start of spring practice, this one has been ready to play. The level of intensity has been consistently high, so when it comes to consistency, this team may be the best we've ever had."

The players saw it.

"In spring drills, our offense had trouble making a first down against us," Morrell remembered. "Then, they made some big plays against Pitt and lit up the scoreboard against Baylor. I said, 'Here we go.'"

Felt, who'd been with Edwards from the beginning, coached the secondary while Ken Schmidt had the outside linebackers and Jim Paronto took the inside linebacker corps. Tom Ramage, another coach who went all the way back with LaVell, handled the defensive line.

Offensively, Roger French coached the offensive line while Mike Holmgren, who later coached with the San Francisco 49ers before taking the Green Bay Packers to a Super Bowl title, tutored the quarterbacks. Norm Chow handled receivers while Lance Reynolds took care of the running backs. Mel Olsen aided French with the offensive front.

Before kickoff at Pitt in the season opener, Edwards knew he had talent but also some question marks, especially opening the season on the road.

BYU definitely was going to be solid on defense, but the offense needed some experience. Bosco had thrown a total of 28 passes while backing up Young in 1983.

"Our main concern was to get through the first four games, not really unbeaten but to have a winning record,

Bosco eyes the Pitt defense, preparing to cap his first BYU start with the winning TD pass to Adam Haysbert.

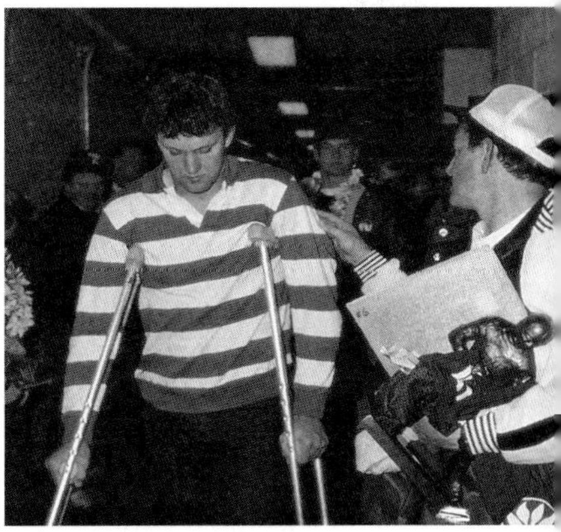

How tough was Robbie Bosco? After directing the Cougars to their biggest bowl victory, the gutty quarterback needed crutches and help from trainer George Curtis just to leave the stadium.

Opponents never got comfortable against the fierce Cougar defense, as Baylor unhappily discovered.

and mainly not to get banged up," Edwards said.

After Pitt, the Cougars would play Baylor, a team that had whipped Young and Co. the previous year.

The next two games were with Tulsa in Provo and Hawaii in Honolulu.

"We did get some people hurt at Hawaii, but then we got a real break, an open date in the schedule," Edwards said. "Had we had a game the week after Hawaii, Bosco would have been out, and so would the team captain, Craig Garrick, in the offensive line.

"But we were very fortunate. In only one game in the whole season did a regular not play. Fortunate, very fortunate."

Pitt was supposed to be the big dog on BYU's schedule. The Panthers were ranked No. 3 in preseason polls and there was plenty of noise coming from the Steel City.

During game week, unranked BYU heard nothing but questions about a couple of Pitt all-Americans, offensive lineman Bill Fralic and pass rusher Chris Doleman.

How could a BYU team without Young and Hudson defeat Pitt with stars like Fralic and Doleman?

Well, it happened, but it probably shouldn't have.

Experience ought to be able to handle youth in the glare of a hyped-up opener, and BYU had lost so many seniors from the '83 team—not just Young and Hudson, but two other offensive starters and linebacker Todd Shell, a first-round draft choice.

Pitt, on the other hand, was coming off an 8–3–1 season, returned 15 starters and was pointing towards a national championship.

Yet the Cougars outplayed Pitt in every phase of the game that Saturday in Pennsylvania.

Unfortuntely, because Bosco threw two third-quarter interceptions that led to quick Pitt touchdowns, the Cougars trailed 14–12 with just 1:40 left in the game.

"I was throwing the ball so badly," Bosco said, "but our defense just kept bailing us out. They kept the score down and kept giving us a chance."

And finally, the Cougars seized on one of those opportunties.

Up in the press box, Norm Chow noticed that Pitt free safety Bill Callahan had been cheating up closer to the line of scrimmage as the game went on. Callahan had no respect for BYU's deep pass.

Of course, the Cougars hadn't really tested Callahan consistently, so he was giving up the deep middle. Earlier in

LaVell Edwards had to feel satisfied while accepting congratulations from Pitt coach Foge Fazio. One national title contender had been eliminated, while another jumped into the running.

By midseason, Robbie Bosco had gone from rookie quarterback to bona fide star.

the game, Bosco took one shot that way, but Callahan intercepted the ball and returned it for a score.

Despite that disaster, the Cougar receivers kept coming to the sideline saying they could make something work going long and to the middle of the field.

Chow decided to do something about it, and phoned down to Holmgren to use the "old 63."

The Cougars had a third and four at the 50-yard line. On this particular play, Kozlowski was the primary receiver and would run a post pattern, while Haysbert played decoy by dragging underneath the Pitt zone.

At the snap, Bosco watched Callahan creep up so he could just follow Kozlowski on the pattern. Bosco also noticed that Haysbert had drawn single coverage by corner Keith Tinsley because Callahan had vacated his deep protection.

It was too good a chance to pass up, so Bosco took one last peek at Haysbert and let it fly.

Haysbert turned upfield, challenging Tinsley as the ball sailed towards them. Haysbert had the angle behind Tinsley and caught a perfect strike, which was amazing enough the way Bosco had been struggling.

Haysbert snatched the ball at the 20 and sprinted untouched for the winning touchdown.

Ultimately, Pitt failed to live up to its preseason billing, something many critics pointed out when attacking BYU's schedule later in the season.

But no matter: The ESPN coverage proved crucial for the Cougars.

"This is the greatest win in the history of the school," Chow told a reporter afterwards. "We won against an experienced team with our young kids."

Given Pitt's failure to match expectations throughout the year, the 1984 opener paralleled BYU's '96 opening win over Texas A&M. In each case, the Cougars toppled a presumed powerhouse on national television and got a jump start on their recognition campaign.

Heading to the home opener against Baylor, BYU entered the AP poll at No. 12—a big, big leap for the Cougars, and a jump that would prove costly to Oklahoma, Washington and Nebraska in late November.

With the Baylor game, the focus turned to Bosco.

At Pitt, he'd started his career from scratch, but completed 25 of 43 passes for 325 yards and a touchdown. He'd been intercepted twice, but he was stepping into a position that had been manned by four consecutive heroes in Young, Jim McMahon, Marc Wilson and Gifford Nielsen.

The Baylor game was Bosco's coming out party in Provo, a place that had come to expect a standard from BYU quarterbacks: 300-yard, three-TD passing performances every time out against anybody this side of the NFL.

Punter Lee Johnson, defensive tackle Jim Herrmann and lineman

Craig Garrick actually talked before the Pitt game about a possible undefeated season.

"Then we put it out of our minds because it was too early," Johnson said. "[But] Pitt carried us the entire season."

Actually, a lot of Cougar fans were thinking about a perfect season—partly because fans just do that naturally but also because the schedule didn't look too menacing if the Cougs somehow could squeeze past Baylor.

No problem: BYU snared the Bears 47–13.

The win over Baylor showed for the first time what could happen when this Cougar team put both offense and defense together on the same day, and it was pretty impressive.

Bosco came out on fire, leading BYU to 21 points in the first quarter on TD passes of 2 and 10 yards to Kozlowski and 39 yards to tight end David Mills.

Overall, Bosco completed 26 of 41 passes for 311 yards and six touchdowns. It was a stunning performance, even by BYU standards.

The waxing of Baylor got even more poll voters' attention, and the Cougars hopped up to No. 8. BYU also got a No. 1 vote in the coaches' poll and continued to receive that same vote every week the rest of the way.

No one ever stepped forward to say he was the guy who was voting BYU No. 1, but Baylor's Teaff was on the panel.

And he'd seen plenty of the Cougars.

Week Three of The Season found many Utahns boasting over the crowning of Miss America, BYU's own Sharlene Wells—ironically, the reigning Holiday Bowl queen.

But now BYU football began to make headlines across the country.

The Cougars owned the nation's longest winning streak at 13 games. Miami, ranked No. 1 when the season started, lost 22–14 to Michigan, ending the previous longest streak.

It was probably about this time that both supporters and skeptics started looking at BYU's schedule to see when the string would run out, and who could make it happen.

It wasn't Tulsa.

In fact, the Golden Hurricane could not get untracked against BYU's defense. Every first-half possession but two were stopped dead by the Cougar defense.

BYU won the game 38–15 as Bosco completed 22 of 33 passes for 314 yards and one touchdown.

Future NFL punter Lee Johnson gave the '84 Cougars good field position all year long.

Linebacker Marv Allen made sure Utah wasn't going to be a threat.

The Cougars led 21–6 at halftime as Vai Sikahema returned a punt 89 yards for a touchdown, Bosco fired a TD shots to Mills and Lakei Heimuli scored on a 1-yard dive.

A vision of the future: Sikahema, used as a reserve running back behind Kelly Smith, ended up earning all-pro honors in the NFL as a punt return star.

Tulsa's inability to move the ball on BYU left a deep impression on coach John Cooper, who called the Cougars "the finest defensive team we have ever played."

Linebacker Marv Allen intercepted two passes against Tulsa, while Jim Herrmann and Kyle Morrell had 11 tackles each. Herrmann added two quarterback sacks.

The Cougars thus climbed to No. 6 in the AP poll and No. 4 in the UPI coaches poll. Ranked ahead of the Cougars in AP were No. 1 Nebraska, followed by Clemson, Texas, Miami and Ohio State. At 3–0, BYU had 817 points in the poll to Ohio State's 860.

Winning a national championship, at least if the team is BYU, takes some luck, the right bounce of the ball, and situations in the polls that just happen to break right.

So far, thing were breaking right.

At Hawaii, though, the Cougars almost went down in flames.

The visit to the islands is always a tough one for the Cougars.

Because of ties to the LDS Church, there are many Polynesian high school players in Hawaii who are BYU fans, and others who just want to escape and get away from home.

For various reasons, BYU always has gotten its share of Hawaiian players, including Kurt Gouveia, Lakei Heimuli and Robert Anae on that '84 team.

Gouveia, a former all-state quarterback and defensive back in Honolulu, turned out to be one of the finest players to ever come out of Hawaii. He later played on Super Bowl teams with the Redskins.

Partly because of all the recruiting raids and partly because the games usually go the same way, University of Hawaii fans can't stand BYU. And the Rainbows get up for the Cougars like no other visitor.

On Sept. 22, the Rainbows went on a mission to halt all this BYU talk and save the country the headache of having ever gotten close enough to sniff the No. 1 ranking.

"I've been saying we've got to take it one game at a time," Hawaii coach Dick Tomey told the local media. "But this game has been building up."

Even Edwards sensed the gravity of the trip to Paradise. "I've been bothered by this trip since last summer," Edwards said. "I was hoping we'd be healthy when we came [to Hawaii].

"I was more concerned with this game than the previous games of the season. They are always great games here, always close. They're so emotional."

Bosco had to play with a pulled hamstring. The Cougars lost offensive

LaVell Edwards holds up the Holiday Bowl trophy as thousands of BYU partisans go crazy. The prize meant a 12–0 season and a national championship for BYU.

guard Randy Rawlinson to a knee injury in the Tulsa game, which meant that Anae would move to center and Matich, who had a bad ankle, would spend some time at guard. Garrick, the best athlete on the offensive line, hurt his toe early in the Hawaii game and that gave the BYU coaches even more personnel miseries.

The Cougars took an early 12–0 lead, but BYU was mistake-prone. There were penalties and dropped passes.

The first touchdown, Kelly Smith's score on a 4-yard run, came after Morrell intercepted a pass. It wasn't a true offensive drive, nothing to give anyone the sense of offensive efficiency. Lee Johnson kicked field goals of 46 and 36 yards.

BYU could have had four touchdowns, but everyone was misfiring and, just as as Edwards had feared, Hawaii was hanging close.

Mark Bellini, one of BYU's great possession receivers, dropped two long passes from Bosco. Kozlowski overthrew Mills on an option pass when Mills was so wide open, he could have run untouched to Pearl Harbor.

Then in the second half, Haysbert appeared to have both hands on a 44-yard bomb at Hawaii's 5-yard line and dropped it.

Omens, every one of them.

Just before halftime, Edwards' concerns came right to the surface. Playing in Hawaii with a kickoff at 10:30 p.m. Provo time, many visiting

Linebacker Kurt Gouveia picked his own particular way to exult in the Cougars' lofty status.

Another throw, another circus catch by Glen Kozlowski, the wide receiver who became known for his acrobatic catches.

BYU's inner circle that perhaps this was a team of destiny.

They had their problems, they hadn't played well. But they had come up with miracles when needed. That kind of thing tends to build momentum and the coaches could feel it.

The Cougars had a bye the following week, allowing for plenty of rest and wound-licking. Even the week off appeared to be a scheduling fluke that was heaven-sent.

BYU stayed at No. 8 in AP and dropped to eighth in UPI.

Remember, though, that some years things just work out right: Without playing a game the week after Hawaii, BYU climbed in the polls when No. 1 Nebraska and No. 2 Clemson both lost.

Now elevated to No. 7 (AP) and No. 6 (AP), the Cougars finally got an easy game out of their systems by clobbering Colorado State 52–9 in Fort Collins.

BYU (5–0) inched up to No. 5 in both polls on Oct. 9. With Texas holding down the top spot, Ohio State lost, which meant only three teams—Boston College, Oklahoma and Washington—stood in the way of a No. 1 ranking with two months left in the season.

Next came Wyoming for BYU's homecoming. This one probably looked like another day at the office on the schedule, but anyone who understands the WAC knows better.

Wyoming and BYU fight like cats and dogs.

No team in the WAC has challenged BYU more than Wyoming through the years. It's a war, pure and simple, and the Cougars found that out on Oct. 14, a Saturday that turned the college football world upside down with upsets.

The Cougars avoided the sword, but just barely, rallying to nudge the Cowboys 41–38. True to the rivalry, BYU needed to score the last eight points to win.

BYU took an early 14–0 lead, but Wyoming closed the gap to 21–20 by going long and deep on the Cougars. That pattern included a successful halfback option pass from Kevin Lowe to Allyn Griffith, who faked out corner Mark Allen.

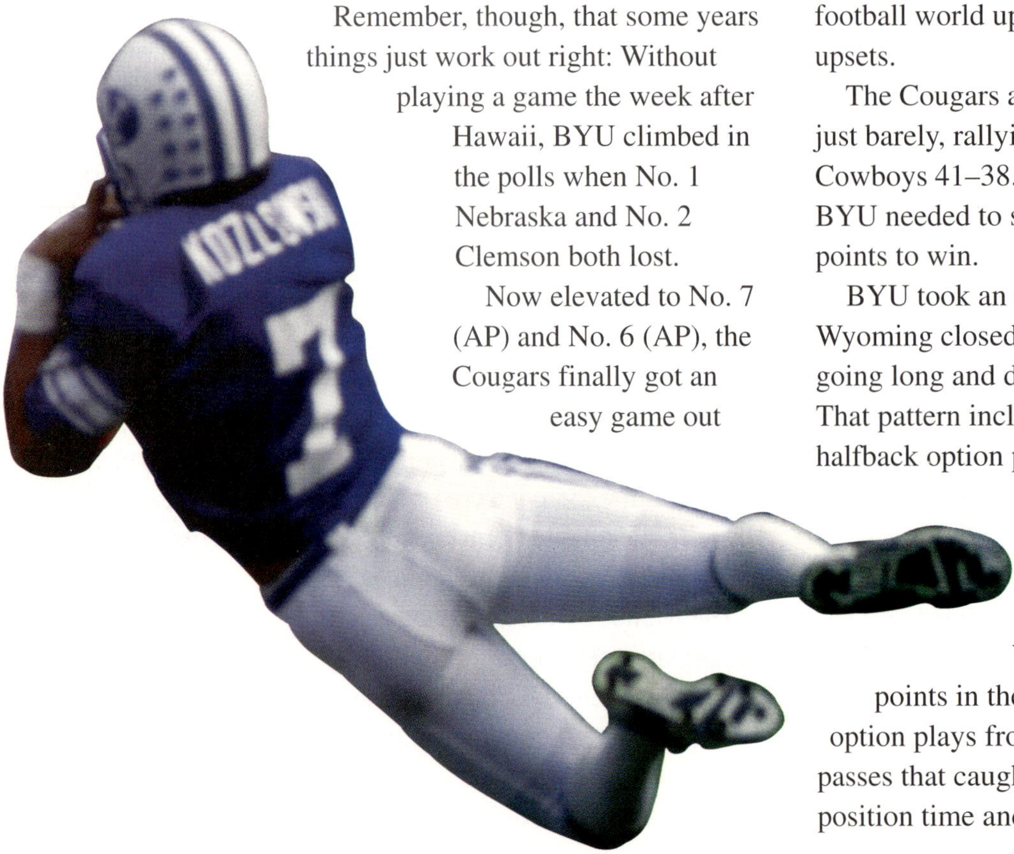

Wyoming scored 18 points in the third quarter, mixing option plays from Scott Runyan with passes that caught the Cougars out of position time and time again.

The Pokes took a 26–21 lead and the two teams traded points the rest of the way.

BYU responded with a Bosco-Heimuli touchdown pass to go up 27–26. Then Wyoming scored on a run by Jeff Westphal.

When a two-point conversion attempt to All-America tight end Jay Novacek failed, Wyoming led 32–27 in the third.

The Cougars answered when Bosco found Mills in the end zone with a 31-yard pass and climbed back ahead 33–32 after a pass conversion failed.

By then it seemed as though the Cougar defense was in tatters. Lowe caught BYU napping and ripped off a 63-yard option run, putting Wyoming back in front 38–33.

This Wyoming-BYU game, like so many before it, had some strange twists. The Pokes tried a quick kick on second down when pinned back deep. The two teams combined to miss six consecutive conversion attempts, five of them in that see-saw third quarter.

One thing was familiar enough about this Cougar–Cowboy matchup, however: It came down to a fourth-quarter alley fight.

The winning touchdown required a nerve-wracking 80-yard drive in 11 plays. During this crucial series of downs, Bosco hit Kozlowski for a completion on fourth and five at the Wyoming 27.

Koz had no recollection of the play, nor his block that helped David Mills haul in the clinching touchdown pass, a 14-yarder from Bosco.

Kozlowski suffered a concussion on the second play of the game and didn't tell anybody about it until afterwards.

How important was avoiding an upset that day in Cougar Stadium?

Well, Oklahoma tied top-ranked Texas 13–13, putting a tarnish on both records. Penn State lost to Alabama, Iowa beat Purdue and George Tech tied with Virginia in a rash of odd top-20 results.

When the polls came out, the Cougars were No. 7 in AP but stayed fifth in UPI. Washington replaced Texas as the top team in the country.

In Seattle, Husky fans were being set up for a big disappointment at the end of the year. And those fans, seething over a No. 1 controversy, nursed an anger that continues today.

Game Seven hatched one more hero for LaVell Edwards.

BYU's pass offense puts a lot of emphasis on the tight end and fullback in addition to the wide receivers. When Steve Young had Gordon Hudson around, the duo lit up defenses and helped set an NCAA record for completion percentage.

Mills appeared from nowhere in BYU's offense in 1984. But without his big plays, his consistent crucial catches, there would be no championship rings on all those fingers.

Nicknamed "Sluggo" by teammates, Mills was a third-stringer behind Hudson and Steve Harper his entire career. He had caught only three passes in three years prior to '84.

Against Wyoming, Mills caught the winning touchdown pass, even though

A happy Glen Kozlowski talks about winning the WAC championship.

BYU had its scary moments during the undefeated '84 season. One of them came during a snowstorm at Air Force, when David Mills caught a game-clinching touchdown pass from Robbie Bosco.

he could not see as blood was flooding his eye after a hit to the head.

In the huddle, he told Bosco he couldn't see. Bosco blew at Mills' eye inside his face mask and the play went as called.

The next week at Air Force, the Cougars not only faced the Falcons but a snowstorm, cold temperatures and a mid-season road trip that many teams just let slip away.

But not BYU.

Not this year.

With the clock winding down to the fourth quarter, Air Force trailed just 21–19, which wasn't all that much of shock. The Falcons had beaten Notre Dame the previous week and were leading the nation in rushing.

Bosco was in the middle of a career day, passing for 484 yards and four touchdowns. But still, the Cougars couldn't shake Air Force.

Then Mills came up with one of his catches.

And the ball wasn't even intended for him, it was meant for Kozlowski. Bosco hurled a post-pattern strike to Koz, but Mills, running a vertical route downfield, had a bead on the ball and adjusted his stride to intersect the throw.

Mills caught the ball in full sprint, cradled it in and raced 25 yards into the end zone. It was a 54-yard touchdown and gave the Cougars a 27–19 advantage.

"We seem to find ways to win," Edwards said afterwards. "They're just different ways."

Mills would go on to catch 64 passes in 1984 for 1,023 yards, but those back-to-back clutch jobs against Wyoming and Air Force kept BYU unbeaten.

Edwards used another trick that day in addition to a lucky catch by the wrong receiver.

The previous week while watching NFL Monday Night football, Edwards saw Green Bay play Denver in the snow. Packer quarterback Lynn Dickey threw for more than 300 yards that night under terrible conditions.

Thinking it might snow in Colorado Springs the following week, Edwards called Green Bay coach Forest Gregg for some tips. Gregg told Edwards that one-cut receiver routes worked well and that receivers running the patterns should cut hard and use a certain type of cleat.

Gregg also suggested that draw plays were effective. Edwards hung up the phone after saying thanks—and put all that information to use in the victory over Air Force.

When the polls came out the following Monday, BYU climbed back to No. 5 in the AP and trailed No. 3 Oklahoma by 18 points in the UPI vote. The sports writers and broadcasters had Nebraska ahead of the Cougars, but the coaches, thanks to that No. 1 mystery vote, kept BYU ahead of the Cornhuskers.

In the preseason, most experts had picked BYU to win its ninth straight WAC title and they penciled in New Mexico to challenge.

After a month of conference games, both were undefeated and the pundits who made the picks looked like geniuses.

Meanwhile, ESPN decided to approach BYU and New Mexico,

asking the schools to change their Saturday game to Thursday night, for a national audience.

Absolutely.

But the great showdown never occurred. BYU thrashed the Lobos 48–0.

The Cougs got the win, the Lobos got the loss, and ESPN's ratings didn't exactly skyrocket during the rout.

BYU scored first. And last. But a key first half 47-yard punt return for a touchdown by Vai Sikahema may have been the turning point. New Mexico seemed to wilt on the spot.

While many viewers may have flipped stations in the route, there were UPI and AP voters who may have stayed on and watched the Cougars because BYU finally started accumulating first place votes.

AP had the 8–0 Cougars No. 4 with four first place votes; UPI placed the Cougars at No. 3 with five ballots for No. 1. Only Texas and Washington were ahead of the Cougars, according to the coaches.

About this time, a debate began. If BYU was this good, shouldn't somebody be looking to get them out of their contract with the Holiday Bowl, which the WAC champion was obligated to attend?

Shouldn't the Fiesta Bowl or Cotton Bowl be able to court the Cougars and provide a solid opponent if BYU did become No. 1?

The argument raged on until the Holiday Bowl officials stepped in and said the paper work was intact and they'd do all they could to provide a proper opponent.

BYU faced UTEP that week.

It was a patsy game, as the Miners were in the midst of a winless season, and the Cougars more or less sleepwalked to a 42–9 decision that clinched at least a tie for the WAC title.

"One thing we had going for us that year that isn't true in 1990s," Bosco recalled, "was the chance to play a couple of games where realistically you knew you were going to win. You hate to call them breathers, but I suppose in a sense, they were."

Sports Illustrated covered the game and produced a six-page, 11-photograph story with an exciting headline: "It's possible: Brigham Young could be No. 1."

Because UTEP was such a pushover, pollsters kept the Cougars at an identical No. 4 spot, but Edwards' team had a 20-game winning streak going, a WAC record.

And the debate raged on.

Edwards is a master at reading his team. He can't always fix their problems, but nothing escapes his eyes. Following the win over UTEP, he sensed a letdown by players at practices leading up to the San Diego State game.

"We've got to keep going," he told the entire team and staff during a meeting. "We've got to take it one game at a time. If we do, good things will happen."

Edwards was not pretending to be a fortune-teller. He was just reading the lines of a script any coach knows by heart. Undefeated seasons and 23-game win streaks do not come along very often in a coach's lifetime.

Against the Aztecs, BYU faced

Safety Kyle Morrell gets a friendly pat from brother Guy, a former Ute, after BYU dispatched Utah.

former offensive coordinator Doug Scovil. And there were some strange feelings about taking on their old mentor.

In San Diego, Aztec fans had learned along with Hawaii, Utah, Wyoming, New Mexico, UTEP and Colorado State to hate the Cougars. The Aztecs and the whole city wanted an upset.

But the contest turned out to be all business for BYU. They were champions, the Aztecs were attempting to avoid a late-season slide, and the difference was obvious.

The Cougars won 34–3.

BYU limited Scovil's offense to just 165 total yards while Bosco and Co. gained a whopping 478.

Afterwards, Scovil offered his opinion of his former team: "This is the best balance between offense and defense I've seen at BYU. Balance-wise, BYU is just the best team we've played all year."

The Cougars got more help that Saturday. No. 1-ranked Washington lost to Southern California and No. 2 Texas fell to Houston.

The Cougars could have moved up to No. 2, but it wasn't to be. They could not get enough points in the polls and voters elected to leapfrog undefeated South Carolina over BYU.

It wasn't fair, but that was the script. It appeared as though at lot of people just did not want *Sports Illustrated*'s headline to come true. How could BYU be No. 1?

BYU ranked third in both polls. Nebraska stood No. 1 despite having a loss, while 9–0 South Carolina now owned the second spot.

During the final week of the most conference seasons—call it rivalry week—just about anything can happen.

And throughout the years, the BYU-Utah series pretty much fell into that category. Which is to say, slightly crazy.

The Cougars knew they'd have a full-scale battle on their hands against the Utes, and they were right. But BYU scratched out a 24–14 victory on a Saturday that was more about survival than style points.

That same day, top-ranked Nebraska lost to Oklahoma 17–7; second-ranked South Carolina bowed to an unimpressive Navy team 38–21. Southern Cal, bound for the Rose Bowl, lost to UCLA 29–10 and Washington struggled to hold off Washington State 38–29.

This was Nebraska's second loss. The Huskers had to fall.

If you were comparing scores, Washington beat WSU by nine, but the Cougars took Utah by 10.

Who knew what the polls might bring?

Bosco completed 27 of 44 passes for 367 yards and three touchdowns against the Utes, but he was intercepted three times, which made the score closer than it should have been—the Cougars had 24 first downs to Utah's 14.

It may not have been a blockbuster score, but it was a win, and over an in-state rival. And a national title was on the line. In that context, the Cougars' triumph—No. 11—was satisfying enough.

Others had faltered. The Cougars had not.

On the way home from the Utah game, BYU players were listening to the Nebraska upset. When announcers counted down the clock, the bus nearly toppled over as players erupted.

There was still some doubt around Provo, and maybe throughout the WAC, about whether poll voters actually would pull trigger and hand BYU the top spot.

Years without respect, not to mention the weird jump by South Carolina so recently, taught everyone not take anything for granted.

But it happened.

BYU was ranked No. 1 in the country in both polls after the victory over Utah.

Whatever the schedule, the Cougars were the only undefeated team in the land. Surprisingly, BYU snagged 40 of 58 first-place votes in the AP poll while Oklahoma had seven.

In the coaches' UPI poll, the Cougars had 30 of 40 first place votes.

"The players held up under adversity," Edwards said after the Utah game. "Anyone can win when everything goes right. It's the teams that can win when things are going wrong that turn out to be champions.

"What made me exceptionally proud today is the fact most of the turnovers came on our end of the field where Utah had great field position, yet they only got seven points out of all of those mistakes, gifts on our part."

To finish No. 1, the Cougars would have to beat Michigan and legendary coach Bo Schembechler in the Holiday Bowl. Bo and LaVell talked about the stakes or the good weather.

But now the pressure truly had been turned up.

The Cougars were No. 1, and the only way they could be voted out was to lose, either in the regular-season finale against 1–9 Utah State or in Holiday Bowl.

A national championship was there for the taking. The air was so thick around Provo, it was getting harder to breathe.

Actually, an upset by Utah State truly was impossible. The Aggies were hopelessly overmatched and went quietly, 38–13, which meant that the Holiday Bowl would be for the whole bag of marbles.

In that final regular-season outing against the Aggies, Bosco completed 26 of 52 passes for 338 yards and a touchdown. It was the end to his first full year as a Cougar starter, a season in which he completed 283 of 458 passes for 3,875 yards and 33 touchdowns. Bosco completed 61 percent of his passes and suffered just 11 interceptions.

Lakei Heimuli led the team in rushing with 796 yards on 158 carries, with nine TDs. The leading receiver ended up being the unsung Mills—60 passes for 1,023 yards and seven touchdowns.

Forget Bo Diddley Tech: The BYU defense startled Michigan with bruising, physical play.

Top: Robbie Bosco got hurt early, left the field, then limped back into the fray, desperate to engineer a Cougar victory.

So it came to payoff time.

The Holiday Bowl.

And remember, when critics of entire bowl structure were trying to pry BYU loose to play in a New Year's Day bowl game, Holiday Bowl reps insisted that they'd find a quality opponent to match the magnitude of the game.

But they couldn't.

Several of the big-name, top-10 teams were asked to buy out of their own committments for a shot at BYU, but nobody bit.

The Holiday Bowl committee met at 10 a.m. on selection day and looked over their options. They immediately put Tennessee and Auburn on hold, believing they could get a more worthy opponent to play the No. 1 team. But nobody wanted the task—or the small paycheck.

"We didn't think money would be as much of a factor and got a rude awakening," Holiday Bowl executive director John Reid said. "We held off some really good teams and they got panicky before we made our decision at 10 p.m.

"From a marquee and tradition standpoint, Michigan was a great opponent."

Michigan?

Almost any other year, Bo Schembechler's Wolverines would have created a marvelous matchup for this WAC upstart trying to win a national title. But in '84, Michigan uncharacteristically had struggled in with a 6–5 record.

So the skeptics got back to howling.

The Holiday Bowl would be played on Friday, Dec. 21, BYU vs. Michigan—more than a week before the New Year's Day bowls with all the "name" schools.

When the entire bowl season was over, preseason No. 1 Auburn won the Liberty Bowl. The other No. 1 team in the early season, Miami, lost in the Fiesta Bowl.

Nebraska, who was perched at No. 1 in November, won the Sugar Bowl while Texas, another No. 1 team in October, lost in the Freedom Bowl.

Washington defeated Oklahoma in the Orange Bowl and made the most noise about not being ranked No. 1.

BYU, meanwhile, had to play first and let everyone else sort it out. And despite the record, Michigan obviously was still Michigan—and nobody's pushover.

The Holiday Bowl figured to be scary, and it was.

Nobody scored in the first quarter. Schembechler's team predictably tried to just hog the ball and the clock.

The big story in the first 15 minutes was a Robbie Bosco pass to Glen

Above: The Wolverines were a rugged and proud bunch, not inclined to let BYU cruise to this momentous victory and proved it by hog-tying Lakei Hemuli.

Left: The Cougar offense found some holes, as Lakei Hemuli burst into the Michigan secondary.

Kozlowski for five yards that got called back on offsetting penalties.

BYU had an illegal shift and Michigan's huge All-American defensive end Mike Hammerstein roughed Bosco on a late hit.

Hammerstein crashed down on Bosco's left leg, and Bosco didn't get up. He rolled over in pain, clutching his left knee to his chest as trainers and medical personnel rushed onto the field.

This was still the first quarter. BYU reserve quarterback Blaine Fowler took sideline instructions and ran onto the field.

Behind BYU's bench, Bosco was carried off the field.

Bosco recalled being carted away: "I thought, here goes the national championship, and all that stuff."

Fowler, meanwhile, completed five of seven passes and managed to keep the ball for nine minutes until the quarter ended with Michigan fielding a punt inside its 20 yard line.

No score. No harm. Just no Bosco.

In the locker room, Bosco asked doctors if he would damage his knee if he played. He was told he could play, but the knee would hurt, feel awkward and stiffen up, especially after a new taping job.

"When it first happened, I didn't think I could return," Bosco said. "But the doctors said it wasn't that bad, and I was able to walk on it a little. If I was able to walk, I knew I would play.

"When you are playing in a big game, you don't feel much pain, as long as you're playing. It hurt on the sideline."

Bosco walked through the tunnel as BYU was getting the ball from Michigan. When fans saw Bosco walking, a big cheer went up, echoing off the walls in Jack Murphy Stadium.

Fowler, who might have done just fine and won the game anyway, walked off.

With Bosco's limited mobility, BYU coaches shifted him into the

On the edge of a championship: Kelly Smith strides through the end zone with a critical touchdown pass.

Assistant coach Roger French and receiver Glen Kozlowski share the joy of it all.

shotgun formation. This changed some of BYU's plays and put pressure on the center and Bosco to deliver and catch the ball.

Bosco would also have to make good, quick decisions because he could not move out of the pocket and scramble to safety easily.

The wounded quarterback engineered an impressive drive after returning. He hit halfback Kelly Smith four times, and even ran the ball, using a baseball slide for a first down and a gain of 13.

Once the Cougars got to the Michigan 5 on a run by Heimuli, Smith scored by cutting inside Michigan's overplaying defense and the Cougars led 7–0 when Lee Johnson added the PAT.

At this point in the game, BYU had a great chance to bust it open and show everyone that even with Michigan not the foe people wanted, the Cougars could spank a Big 10 team just as easily as one from the WAC.

Michigan's offense could not get anything going and when punter Monte Robbins attempted to kick under pressure from BYU's rush inside his 17, he fumbled the ball and linebacker Ladd Akeo pounced on it at the 5-yard line.

A rout was so close that BYU fans could smell it.

But it was not to be. Bosco needed more stage time.

On a third and two, BYU called a naked reverse play with Bosco keeping the ball. As he made a pivot, Bosco lost his grip and the ball dribbled into the end zone, where Michigan recovered.

Rout off, game on.

The Wolverines promptly scored after a long drive, but got two breaks along the way—including losing a pitch that appeared to be recovered by BYU before going out of bounds.

Michigan appeared to settle for a field goal, but a roughing-the-kicker call on BYU gave Schembechler a second chance at a touchdown.

It paid off as halfback Rick Rogers scored, tying the game at 7–7.

BYU then drove 60 yards to set up Johnson's 31-yard field goal, giving the Cougars a 10–7 halftime lead.

"I knew my field goal was clutch," Johnson said. "I had to make it. I realized what was at stake, but I felt very confident it had to be made. When it went through, I remembered Hammerstein saying something, but you can't print it."

Bowl games and BYU just don't go together without maddening turnovers that make games closer than they should be—or even losses that shouldn't happen. And that was the case again for the Cougars in this brightest spotlight of all.

It was almost a comedy of errors.

BYU gave up the football four times, three fumbles and an interception. The Cougars also had a field goal

Excitement reigns as the Cougars celebrate the winning score, a sight Cougar fans never will forget.

blocked. If this was a high-powered offense—and it was—those possessions likely would have produced 21 points or more.

The Cougars got zilch.

But Michigan scored on a 10-yard pass from Chris Zurbrugg to Bob Perryman in the third and led 14–10.

If losing the lead wasn't enough for Edwards on a very frustrated sideline, the quarter ended with BYU's turnover, setting up Michigan just 11 yards from a touchdown.

Backed against the wall, the Cougar defense once again rose up and forced a field goal by Tod Schlopy which gave Michigan a 17–10 lead with just over 14 minutes to play.

Right at that moment, it looked as though all those skeptics might have the last laugh.

The Cougars, though, refused to be licked—even by their own mistakes. As Edwards preaches so often, they just kept playing.

Thus the final quarter in Holiday Bowl VII was one of the finest, guttiest performances in BYU football history. Never had so much been on the line under such difficult circumstances.

Credibility, recognition, perfection, a season of triumph and pain were on the line.

And this amazing team came through.

Bosco completed seven passes to

Linebackers Kurt Gouveia and Leon White in their proudest moment as Cougars.

five different receivers in the quarter, including a throw that Kozlowski grabbed while defying the laws of physics.

From the Michigan 7-yard linc, Bosco looked things over and spotted Kozlowski in the back of the end zone. He fired a strike between two Michigan defensive players, and everybody went up for the ball.

Somehow, some way, Kozlowski came down with it—while landing flat on his back on the turf.

That score tied things at 17-all and capped an 80-yard drive that took 3:23. When Johnson kicked the PAT, 10:51 remained on the clock.

BYU's defense stuffed Michigan, a smash-mouth team that managed just 124 yards rushing. But then Bosco was intercepted trying to throw to Kozlowski, and Jim Scarcelli returned the ball to the Cougar 45.

Adversity once again was all over the Cougars. Pressure hung in the stadium like a thick cloud.

So one more time, the BYU defense stood up. Kyle Morrell (11 tackles) was sensational and Kurt Gouveia chipped in with a 16-yard sack to kill Michigan's last serious threat of the game.

Title time.

Bosco led the Cougars downfield, slicing apart Michigan's tiring defense. He even limped his way to several gains.

Then from the 13-yard line, dodging a rush and stepping up into the pocket, Bosco flung a pass to Smith, who hauled in the ball standing up for the game-winner.

Smith had been double covered on the play. But when he saw Bosco scramble out of a tackle, he changed direction, and suddenly he was open.

Bosco made the read and the delivery.

Smith, who later became a coach at Dixie College in southern Utah, had been a solid safety valve receiver all season long. A player with exceptional speed, he was tough to cover coming out of the backfield.

And now Michigan, with all its defensive stars, found out the hardest way of all.

The crowd went crazy, piling down onto the turf, celebrating BYU's victory, its 13th of the season and 23rd in a row.

Everyone had a hand in the victory, but oh, that defense. Michigan actually lost three yards on offense for the entire fourth quarter, winding up with a paltry total of 202.

The Cougars had 255 yards total offense—in the fourth quarter alone—and Bosco was 12 of 14 in that magnificent stretch run. He finished with 30 of 42 passing for 343 yards and two touchdowns despite the bum leg.

Lee Johnson, a punter and kicker who would go on to an NFL career that spanned two decades, punted only once in the game.

National TV zooms in on the undefeated Cougars.

"It's amazing," Edwards said afterwards. "If somebody would have told me we would turn the ball over six times and win, I'd have told them they were crazy. But we did it and this has been the trademark of this team all season.

"I've seen it all as far as quarterback performances as far as BYU goes. He was in tremendous pain, but I can't think of a better quarterback performance than Bosco's tonight."

That 1984 team continued to produce after its championship season.

The squad produced at least six lawyers, four graduate students who earned master degrees, 15 NFL draftees, one physician, one evangelical minister and four coaches—including Bosco.

More than a decade after winning the mythical national championship by being No. 1 in both polls, players and coaches from the '84 team still get questioned about that season.

"I quit defending it," Johnson said. I'm a believer."

And why not?

Those Cougars made believers of everyone on the football field.

They never lost, and they've got the trophy to prove it.

C H A P T E R

THREE

Nestled against a backdrop of majestic mountains, BYU is the largest private university in the nation, with huge towering buildings, a law school, and support services to rival a small city.

3

The Little Team

"Like many of their contemporaries, the founders of Brigham Young Academy [in the late 1800s] believed that competitive sports both detracted students from academic work and threatened the tranquility of their community."

– Gary James Bergera and Ron Priddis, historians

That Couldn't

STROLL ACROSS THE CAMPUS at Brigham Young University.

The sidewalks look scrubbed. Flower planters are immaculately groomed. The grass is always cut, and if you were given a dollar for every scrap of garbage or paper you could find just lying around, you'd starve to death.

With huge towering buildings, a law school, and support services to rival a small city, BYU is the largest private university in the nation. Owned and operated by the Church of Jesus Christ of Latter-day Saints, BYU has an enrollment of more than 26,000 students.

Near the entrance to campus, along Canyon Road in Provo, stands Cougar Stadium, voted one of the top 10 scenic venues in college football.

With Mt. Timpanogos forming a majestic backdrop, the 65,000-seat stadium has been the scene of some of the NCAA's most thrilling football games—and home to some of the best college quarterbacks of all time.

In the western United States, only the University of Washington regularly draws more fans to watch college football. Arizona State is a close third.

But in the Rockies, Provo is the place where quarterbacks go to become heroes, where records fall, and where coach LaVell Edwards has built a legendary program by implementing what later became known as the West Coast offense.

Enlarging the stadium and scheduling nationally known teams like Notre Dame, Penn State and Miami officially made BYU a football powerhouse. Crowds of more 65,000 now regularly flock to Provo to watch the sport that once was banned from campus.

BYU's athletic teams consistently are ranked among the nation's best for all-sport excellence. Year in and year out, the Cougars rank in the nation's top 20 in NCAA intercollegiate programs.

Following the improbable national championship of 1984, church and university officials were shocked at how much publicity the football team generated. In terms of positive public relations, BYU could not have purchased enough advertising to equal the exposure the school received.

Ironically, however, BYU has a long history of ambivalence toward competitive sports. At times, it's seemed like a love-hate relationship.

As for football, well, BYU managed a good part of this century without accomplishing much of anything on the gridiron. And no one acted particularly distressed over it.

Most football powers of the current era have deep roots, thundering tradition, nationally known fight songs, long-standing fan support, staggering history.

BYU has, well . . .

Let's just say there are aren't many parallels between the origins of football at BYU and Notre Dame.

"Like many of their contemporaries, the founders of Brigham Young Academy [in the late 1800s] believed that competitive sports both detracted students from academic work and threatened the tranquility of their community," wrote historians Gary James Bergera and Ron Priddis.

Still, students organized sports clubs and activities in the early years, including the intramural Baseball Club in 1891—the first athletic organization of any kind at the Academy.

The school's initial administrative action regarding athletics came in 1905, when the school hired Clayton Teetzel, a non-Mormon coach from Michigan, who had played football and ran track in college.

Soon afterwards, BYA offered classes in physical education, including classes with "free-arm movements and dumb-bell drills" for both men and women.

In the late 1890s, BYA fielded a football team. The rules of the game were not well defined in those days and several games ended in fights. When BYA formed a team in 1896 to play the University of Utah, the game ended in a brawl which had to be broken up by police.

On Christmas Day the following year, a BYA football game with Crescent High in Salt Lake City ended in a slugging match when BYA took the lead in the second half.

George Goddard, who was then superintendent of the church's Sunday School Union, complained to LDS President Wilford Woodruf that "drinking, profanity, and fighting" were so common at football games that it was tough to properly oversee the activity.

Goddard said he "could not find one particle of good arising from indulgence in either yells or football games, but saw a great amount of evil."

Karl G. Maeser statue in front of Maeser Building.

Two years later, with continued problems, the church's board of education—presided over by former BYA principal and Superintendent of Chruch Schools Karl G. Maeser—made it official. Football was banned at all church schools.

Maeser labeled it "a barbarous, brutal exercise not to be dignified by the title of game."

That edict later was adjusted to allow each school to determine its own policy about sports in general, but football was still outlawed.

Academy students did an end-around by forming their own club teams in Provo and wore BYA uniforms for games that drew enthusiastic crowds.

One of the captains of those unsanctioned teams was Eugene Roberts, who later became BYU's athletic director and track coach and one of the most influential figures—not only at the university, but in sports history in the state of Utah.

B.Y.A
B.Y.A
R.G
B.Y.A

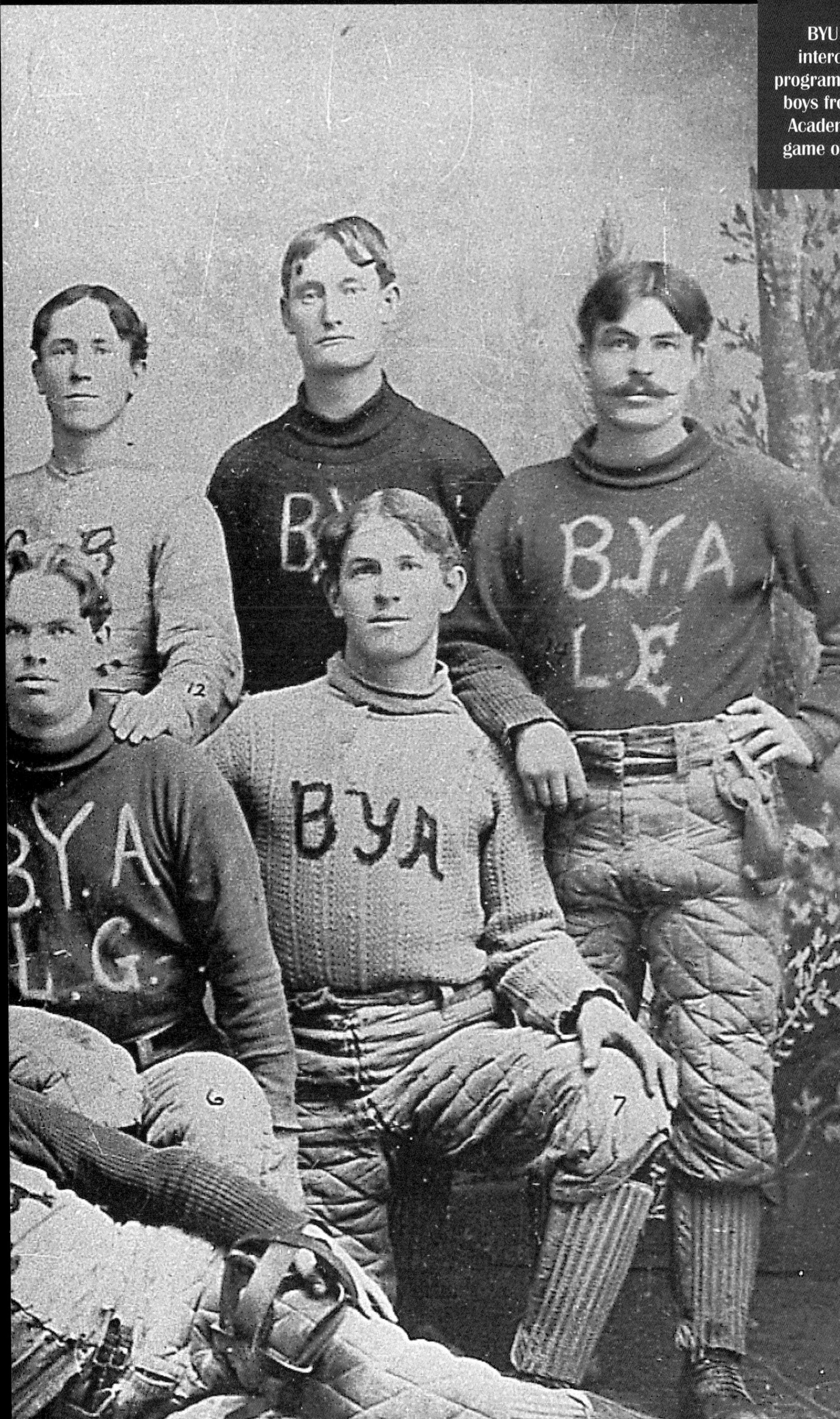

BYU didn't begin an intercollegiate football program until 1922, but the boys from Brigham Young Academy were trying the game on for size in 1897.

Even when football was banned and then reinstated as a full-time sport at BYU, it wasn't exactly big-time. It didn't take many fans to create a full house in the old days.

The ban on football was lifted by the church in 1921.

To be fair to early BYU administrators, it should be noted that football was also banned at times during the early part of the century at schools such as Columbia and Stanford after 18 deaths were reported from football activity nationwide in 1905.

When the Academy became BYU and then-president Frankline D. Harris pledged to "exert every effort and endeavor to make football the major sport at the Y," BYU nonetheless won an average of just three games per season for the next 15 years.

A member of the Rocky Mountain Conference (then called the Skyline Conference) BYU football was not a force.

In 1928, students raised money to build a football stadium on the current site of the Richards physical education building. The bleachers would be situated on the side of the hill, just below the present faculty office buildings.

There was criticism when students donated two days of work towards the stadium because what was needed was a team that would attract patrons to the new seats—not seats for those who had never attended games.

BYU's first facilities for athletics had five showers for 400 athletes in track, basketball and football.

It would be 23 years until a stadium and locker room facilities were built and even minimum facilities were available for university sports.

Undaunted, BYU and its student body of just 2,000 joined the Skyline Conference with Utah, Wyoming, Colorado, Denver University and Colorado Agricultural College.

From the beginning of the football program in 1922, BYU managed just two winning seasons in its first decade. In one stretch against rival Utah, BYU did not score a single point through 15 games.

The first victory over Utah didn't come until 1942—Ute fans dismiss it as a War Year—and even then, the feat was repeated only one other time in conference history.

In 1949, BYU was labled as the "losingest" team in the nation by a national broadcaster.

BYU lost to both the University of Pacific and Kansas State in 1963, which was a fairly remarkable double, since neither of those teams won another game.

The teams weren't all that good in the late 1930s, but no one could accuse BYU of having dull uniforms. That's Lloyd Brink (left) and Art Gilbert looking ready to rumble in their striped jerseys.

A Denver University student newspaper, *The Clarion,* ran an editorial that delievered the ultimate insult: "Let's beat someone besides BYU or let's give up football."

Postscript: DU couldn't beat anyone else and did give up football.

One of the big problems during this dark era for BYU was the school's lack of financial support, not to mention the absence of grants-in-aid for athletes and a failure to actively recruit around the country.

It wasn't until the late 1950s—and the hiring of Hal Kopp—that BYU made strides to play with the big boys. Money finally became available for educational assistance and adequate pay for coaches. Lo and behold, Kopp managed to post a 13–14–3 record in three seasons from 1956–58. Those numbers might not sound impressive,

Dave Chadwick looked fierce enough in this running pose from 1947, but no one outside Utah was paying much attention to BYU football.

but at BYU, anything close to .500 was a success.

Following Kopp's tenure, things turned bleak again. Tally Stevens went 6–15 over two years, then former player Hal Mitchell was 8–22 from 1961–63.

In the final year of Mitchell's stay, though, BYU joined the Western Athletic Conference—perhaps the biggest step of all toward ultimate football respectability.

Mitchell did make one other sensational move, though no one could have guessed the consequences at the time. He hired a Salt Lake City high school coach to be one of his assistants.

Fellow named LaVell Edwards.

Tommy Hudspeth came from the Canadian Football League to take over in 1964, and after one desultory 3–6–1 season, the Cougars managed to win the WAC in '65—though their overall record was a less-than-sensational 6–4.

Still, BYU had shown it was serious about football. Preparing for life in the WAC, Hudspeth and his staff—notably holdovers Chris Apostol and Edwards—ventured out for some serious recruiting.

By the late 1960s, coach Tommy Hudspeth was trying to put BYU football on the map. Hudspeth won the school's first WAC title and molded the ideas of a good assistant named LaVell Edwards. The staff (from left): Edwards, John Payne, Hudspeth, Wayne Startin, Earl Lindley and Chris Apostol.

BYU began recruiting some ex-military players in the '60s, and one of them, Phil Odle (88), became the school's leading career pass-catcher.

Cougar football began to go big-time with the elevation of LaVell Edwards to head coach in 1972 and a series of bold strokes by dynamic athletic director Glen Tuckett.

That summer, Edwards snagged a quarterback named Virgil Carter. Apostol returned from a cross-country tour with some U.S. Marines, servicemen who had played football and were due for release.

One of these Marines was Phil Odle, who became the all-time leading receiver in school history. Carter ended up breaking two NCAA passing records before being drafted into the NFL and playing with the Cincinnati Bengals.

The energy provided by Hudspeth, the retaining of Edwards and the influx of football talent to Provo jump-started Cougar football.

It turned out to be the foundation of one of the most potent offensive arsenals in college football history.

Another man figured prominently in this transformation at BYU: Glen Tuckett, a baseball coach who became athletic director, helped shape BYU's football program into a national powerhouse.

Tuckett oversaw important schedule changes and expansion of Cougar Stadium from 35,000 to 65,000 seats in 1983.

With his connections to college bowls, major conferences, coaching legends like Joe Paterno, Bobby Bowden and Lou Holtz, Tuckett found a way to squeeze BYU into games and bowls.

Tuckett also had the vision to understand what BYU football could mean to the community and the LDS Church.

Unfortunately, the Tuckett saga did not have an entirely happy ending. Forced to leave BYU at the mandatory retirement age of 65, this still-capable administrator immediately was scooped up by the University of Alabama, which was facing a ton of trouble from the NCAA and might have lost its football program entirely.

Tuckett spearheaded a plan that not only saved football, but softened penalties and proved to the NCAA that the university had regained institutional control over its favorite sport.

Even with Tuckett gone from BYU, however, football was on the permanent fast track in Provo.

By the mid-1970s, Edwards had begun the remarkable run that has carried BYU to a national championship, to its 14–1 season and Cotton Bowl victory in 1996 and a staggering string of WAC titles.

And the university has discovered that football and spiritual-based

By the early 1980s, BYU had achieved enough success and acquired such a football following that plans were drawn up for a huge expansion of Cougar Stadium.

education can co-exist quite happily, indeed.

Several times during BYU's early struggles, LDS authorities made references to how important sports could be in the church's missionary effort – opening doors and offering exposure.

After BYU's first bowl appearance under Edwards in 1974—a loss to Oklahoma State in the Fiesta Bowl—LDS Apostle Marvin J. Ashton noted when BYU's players dug in and played harder, it was impressive and turned out to be a "good missionary tool."

This belief was re-emphasized in 1995 when the university hired Rondo Fehlberg, a former All-American wrestler at BYU, to replace Tuckett as athletic director.

Fehlberg, an attorney and vice-president of the energy giant Pennzoil prior to the call back to Provo, promptly took over as a combination cheerleader, administrator, preacher, peacemaker, fund-raiser, you name it.

At a Cougar Club meeting during

his first autumn as athletic director, Fehlberg decided to fire up the natives, hyping his vision of what BYU sports should represent. He fired up some of the gray-haired fellows so much that one man jumped to his feet and proclaimed: "You've got me so excited, I'm ready to climb Mt. Timp right now."

In October 1995, when the athletic department featured a Midnight Madness for students, Fehlberg had breakfast in Moscow that same morning. He hopped on a Pennzoil private jet and walked into the Smith Fieldhouse that evening in time for the Madness festivities.

Since coming to Provo from the Houston area, Fehlberg has infused the program with the attitude of an outsider, poking around BYU's athletic closets from inside out. He sees things differently, listens a little differently and talks a little differently than what the athletic department has become accustomed to through the decades.

"He certainly hit the ground running," Edwards said. "He has a lot of enthusiasm. He's been very good at relying on people around him, like assistant athletic director Pete Witbeck, for things he is not familiar with. And he's good at how he approaches people. He is also very methodical."

In a nutshell, Fehlberg believes BYU should be viewed in the same light as Notre Dame. And be just as successful.

Sensing a need to rekindle interest in all aspects of BYU athletics, the kind of fire experienced in the early '80s, Fehlberg created a vision and then shared it with fans—in group meetings throughout Utah and beyond. A cassette tape containing Fehlberg's message was sent to fans worldwide.

One preliminary building block in Fehlberg's approach is admitting to BYU fans that the school has made some mistakes. Indeed, in some cases, really blown it.

This refreshing "coming down off

A new era began in 1995 when former BYU wrestler Rondo Fehlberg took over as athletic director and worked with Edwards towards the goal of keeping Cougar football in national headlines. By the end of '96, Fehlberg and Edwards were celebrating a 14-1 season, the most victories ever in a year by a Division I school.

the mountain" approach immediately perked up a lot of people around BYU. No one was used to hearing too many confessions coming from university administrators.

Fehlberg also set out to broach the huge chasm that had developed between athletics and the school's academic community, and some of his early efforts had immediate impact.

The athletic director has promised changes. "We'll kill some sacred cows out there; and we'll eat some others," he said.

Fehlberg bangs away on several themes, everything from improving facilities to relentless recruiting inside and outside the LDS faith and even the controversial issue of possibly changing conference affiliation.

One thing obvious about all of it, though, is that BYU sports—and football in particular—is big-time.

Really big-time.

From the days of the leather helmet, broken noses and a joke of a program, BYU has lifted itself over the past 30 years into a respected college football program.

Nobody's talking about banning the sport anymore.

How times have changed at the old Academy.

Half

Time

BYU
BYU

COUGARS

BRIGHAM YOUNG UNIVERSITY
KSL 1160
SOUTHWEST AIRLINES

30

HOLIDAY BOW

LAMB
WAC
WAC
WAC
14

BYU
80

MAHON
9
WILSON
6
14
12

CHAPTER

FOUR

After 26 seasons and more than 230 wins at BYU, Edwards ranks among the top echelon of all college coaches.

4

The Only Mormon

"THE WAY HE HANDLES YOUNG MEN IS OUTSTANDING. HE'S HONEST AND PATIENT . . . AND TEACHES THAT THERE'S MORE TO LIFE THAN FOOTBALL AND THAT, IN MY OPINION, SEPARATES HIM FROM OTHER COLLEGE COACHES."

—DICK FELT
BYU ASST. COACH

Coaching the Single Wing

LAVELL EDWARDS and his wife Patti once accepted an invitation from their friend Sy Kimball to go fishing in Alaska.

Edwards likes to fish, but it isn't that big a deal and Kimball, a longtime aficionado from numerous trips deep sea fishing off Baja, wanted the trip to be a special experience for his buddy the coach.

The first morning, Kimball waited for Edwards to arise, and finally had to wake him up. Not exactly raring to go, LaVell would have slumbered through the entire outing.

Once onboard and out on the water, everyone got outfitted with tackle, poles and gear but the salmon weren't biting. After a long wait, Kimball noticed LaVell's pole appeared to be wiggling. He nudged the coach and asked him to test the line. Sure enough, Edwards had a lunker.

Kimball tells this story with a laugh because LaVell Edwards is a man who so easily loved and such a magnet for success—for instance, the way that big fish came calling for the guy who was barely interested.

That's the type of banter that follows Edwards, who in his own part of the world (and a few others) is a walking, breathing legend.

LaVell Edwards often looks glum and occasionally downright angry, but Cougar players, coaches and fans know his inside warmth. Sometimes it just doesn't show.

"He is like a father to the players," offered Steve Sarkisian, who quarterbacked Edwards' 1996 team to a 14–1 record. "He really cares about us individually, and while he's low-key and sometimes looks like he's bored in games, nobody wants to win more than he does. He has a fire inside of him and he loves the game."

After 25 seasons and more than 225 wins at BYU, Edwards ranks among the top echelon of all college coaches—trailing only Bo Schembechler, Tom Osborne, Woody Hayes, Bobby Bowden, Joe Paterno, Amos Alonzo Stagg, Pop Warner and Bear Bryant.

"LaVell's consistency from one year to another has been incredible and unbelievable," said in-state rival Ron McBride from the University of Utah.

Consider some amazing stretches: From the time he took over at BYU in 1973 through thc 1985 scason, Edwards' teams won 122 games while losing only 36. From 1979 through '85, the Cougars were 77–12 and bagged seven consecutive conference championships.

Over two and a half decades, Edwards' teams averaged nine wins per season. He has coached 26 first team All-Americans, four Davey O'Brien award-winning quarterbacks and a Heisman Trophy recipient, Ty Detmer.

In one of his most unusual, yet noteworthy achievements, Edwards saw one of his former players on the NFL's Super Bowl championship team every year from 1980 to 1992. Oh, and flash forward to the '97 Super Bowl: Green Bay coach Mike Holmgren was a former BYU assistant and likewise current Packer quarterback coach Andy Reid.

History will underscore in years to come that Edwards was a man with a golden touch.

Don't forget Sy Kimball's fish story.

LaVell Edwards never has held a job outside of the state of Utah. His first stop was Salt Lake City's Granite High, where he struggled through eight seasons without a winning record.

Edwards then was hired as an assistant at BYU by Hal Mitchell.

> "LaVell's really happy. He just forgot to tell his face."
>
> – Karl Tucker
> Former BYU
> Golf Coach

Edwards is now a coaching legend, admired by his peers across the nation. Men like Jimmy Johnson, (left) now with the Miami Dolphins, and Washington coach Jim Lambright were respectful opponents.

"They wanted somebody with experience running the single wing," Edwards joked, "and I was the only Mormon around still using it."

But the idea of taking a unique offense nobody else used and making it work by catching opponents off stride stuck with Edwards. Future Cougar foes would discover that the old single wing proponent had another surprise in store for them.

College football in the 1940s, '50s and '60s was dominated by schools like Alabama, Ohio State, Notre Dame, Penn State, Michigan and Texas. These schools simply grabbed the top athletes around, put them on the field and waited for the scoreboard to light up. It was a time of power football: Run left, run right and run up the middle. A pass was an option most teams avoided whenever possible.

Ohio State's crusty old Hayes once uttered the gospel of most coaches, announcing: "When you throw a pass, only three things can happen and two of them are bad."

But out in the wilds of Utah, LaVell Edwards understood from the beginning that for the underdogs, those teams that couldn't recruit or compete toe-to-toe with the big-name powerhouses, there had to be an alternative.

Teams with less resources, fewer stars and practically no depth needed a ploy, some kind of gimmick offense that could partially level the playing field.

Mitchell's single wing failed because there were not enough young high school players experienced enough to run it. And Mitchell only lasted three years as head coach, so the thing never had a chance to take root.

The single wing called for a direct snap from center to a single running

The man known simply as "LaVell" throughout Utah is a master communicator, whether he's addressing a bowl game press conference, making a point with one of his players or chatting with TV interviewer Lesley Visser.

back and it had worked as late as the 1950s. Mitchell wanted to bring it back in the '60s and force opponents to have to prepare for something odd during game week, thus giving BYU some kind of edge. Ironically, the same philosophy has recycled itself with the wishbone offense in the 1990s, as undersized, depth-poor teams like Army, Air Force and Rice have enjoyed considerable success by employing an unusual style and becoming comfortable with it.

Edwards never forgot that idea, even if the single wing did not catch on.

The single wing showed signs of promise under Mitchell when Eldon Fortie ran himself into BYU's record book and by carrying the ball 199 times for 1,149 yards. Fortie averaged 5.8 yards per carry, best in the WAC. He was from Granite High—that's right, Edwards' old school. Mitchell didn't last long at BYU, but he impressed Edwards. Mitchell was intelligent and he was a visionary man who looked to make the game better.

Edwards recalled that Mitchell used to sit around and say to other coaches, "I'll tell you guys, one day BYU is going to be a great football school."

But just not quite yet.

Mitchell's replacement was Canadian Football League coach Tommy Hudspeth, another boss Edwards found refreshing, smart and a good talker—especially the areas of recruiting and developing talent.

Hudspeth led BYU to its first conference championship using a different sort of strategy, the passing game. California import Virgil Carter was given the green light to turn the ball loose, and Edwards watched in fascination.

Then in 1972, Hudspeth was let go and the BYU administration turned the reins over the old single wing master from Granite High.

Needless to say, Cougar football has never been the same.

Edwards took over the head coaching job with plenty of perspective about the university, about football and why there seemed to be so much negativity surrounding the program.

Coaching staffs had become revolving doors. There was no continuity. Everybody expected BYU to lose and people would sit around and make excuses.

Edwards heard the old lines: BYU had too many Mormon missionaries and so the Cougars must be soft. Or that you couldn't win because the school was owned and operated by the LDS Church, and therefore non-Mormons never would be successfully recruited.

Another excuse was lack of resources; for instance, in terms of staff numbers. BYU had six coaches, while rivals Utah and Utah State employed eight apiece.

All the so-called reasons BYU couldn't win just piled up, and Edwards finally got tired of hearing them.

"What we tried to do was turn the negative things into positives," Edwards said. "We looked at the opposite side of all the old arguments."

But LaVell was no dreamer looking for a place on the throne.

Hardly.

"I had no grandiose plan in place that gray night in January of 1972 when I said yes," Edwards said of his hiring. "In no way, shape or form was my head filled with a master scheme that would revolutionize the program, the region, and the game.

"I had not planned and plotted my entire life with an eye focused on the fateful day when a college program would be mine and I could finally put all my ideas to the test."

LaVell Edwards learned a lot of his values from the man who turned into one of his biggest fans, his father Philo.

No, it was more basic than that: Edwards simply enjoyed coaching. He liked teaching young men, watching them learn and play while improving. That basic nature in the man speaks volumes about his foundation for success.

Now the winningest football coach in the western United States, Edwards had deep roots right in BYU's back yard. His parents, Philo and Addie were salt of the earth, God-fearing simple people who taught basic principles of honesty, charity and ethics.

In 1984, Philo Edwards stood up on his old legs before a church group and bore a golden testimony before his neighbors—thanking his maker and expressing love for his petite wife Addie, 87, and for his full life and his 12 children.

Included among those children was No. 7, the celebrated LaVell.

A big, handsome, athletic-looking man, Philo told church members he

Edwards wasn't always so grumpy-looking. Back in 1977, he looked downright cheery—well, almost.

Everyone wants to talk to LaVell, even on the field. BYU Network announcer Greg Wrubell gets the latest scoop.

Right: There's no question about LaVell's popularity . . . he's even been a magazine poster boy.

had experienced so much in his life to be thankful for. And there were things he hoped to still do in his lifetime.

Afterward a neighbor asked Philo exactly what he would want before he died. "I'd like to see my boy win a national championship," he replied.

From late autumn on, in a small Orem neighborhood called Vineyard, that wish became known as "The Philo Syndrome."

And piece by piece, it came true.

When title contenders Nebraska, Oklahoma, South Carolina and Washington lost games that year, insiders nodded and assumed it was the syndrome at work. Ditto when BYU finally made it to No. 1 in the polls, and again when the Cougars whipped Michigan in the Holiday Day in December.

When Philo was confronted inside the confines of the family's simple furnished apartment and asked for an explanation of this phenomenon, the elder Edwards turned to Addie, and in classic family tradition, attributed the whole affair to his wife.

Someone else. A complete transfer of credit. It was the Edwards way.

That national championship—Philo Syndrome or whatever—was directed by a man his friends and coaching peers insist will not boast about himself, a man almost devoid of ego in a business where self-promotion is coin of the realm.

"Everyone out there knows what LaVell's accomplished," former Syracuse coach Dick MacPherson said. "He's done the impossible."

Baylor coach Grant Teaff singled out Philo and Addie's boy LaVell as one of the three top technical minds in college football.

Teaff, who was named the national college coach of the year in 1975, insisted Edwards deserved that same honor for 1984—but had been earning the award for some time.

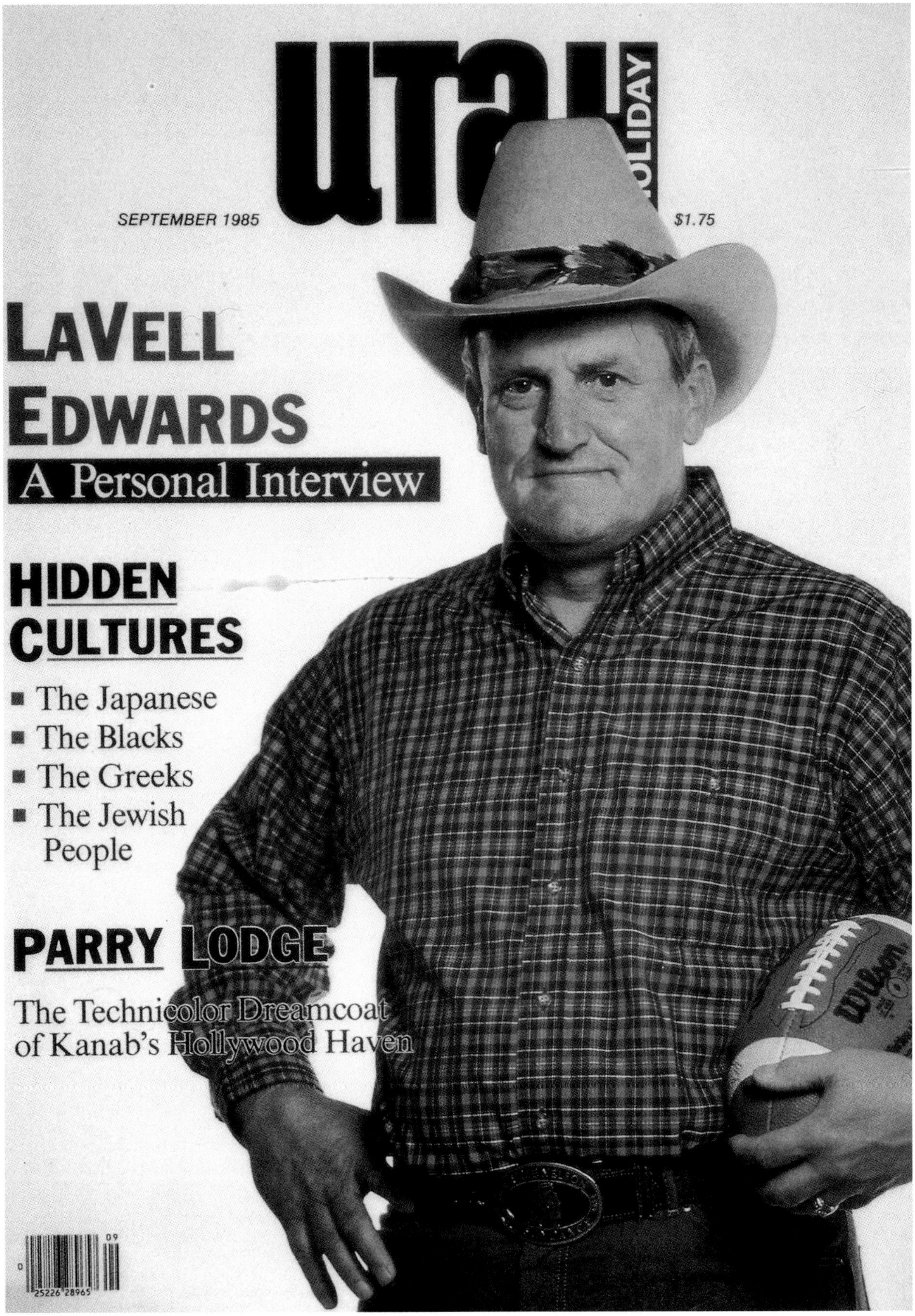
UTAH HOLIDAY
SEPTEMBER 1985
$1.75
LAVELL EDWARDS
A Personal Interview
HIDDEN CULTURES
▪ The Japanese
▪ The Blacks
▪ The Greeks
▪ The Jewish People
PARRY LODGE
The Technicolor Dreamcoat of Kanab's Hollywood Haven

Edwards has inspired loyalty, and not just from players and fans. Five of his assistants (from left) Norm Chow, Lance Reynolds, Tom Ramage, Roger French and Ken Schmidt have stood at LaVell's side for at least 15 seasons each.

"I will be very disappointed if he is not coach of the year. It would be a fitting tribute to a great man, team and season," Teaff said. The American Football Coaches Association did name Edwards as their coach of the year in early January of 1985.

"He is one of the most honest men I've known," Teaff said. "And you can't separate the coaching from the man."

It also could be said that you can't separate the man from his roots.

Philo and Addie owned 80 acres in Buckhorn but decided to move. But they couldn't sell, trade or give the land away until someone finally agreed to pay Philo $10 an acre. He took the $800 and put a down payment on a 17-acre Orem orchard.

Being from a big family did not exempt LaVell from chores. He learned to work early in life, often drawing cow-milking duties and a lot of fruit-picking chores.

"I would say LaVell grew up a solid boy," Philo said. "He loved his family and was taught faith and prayer. He prays in the locker room with his team before every game.

"I worked around him and never heard him use any slang."

Both parents insisted that their famous son never got caught up in his own notoriety. Quite the opposite.

"We have to ask him point blank to find out what's going on with the football team," Philo said.

The family also told a story about a near-disaster in LaVell's youth.

"I just bought a new Roadmaster Buick. We always had trucks but only one car, and I let LaVell take it one night for a date with some of his friends. I was in the hospital," Philo Edwards said.

The young LaVell was traveling with a carload of friends and approached the overpass near Pleasant Grove when just in time he noticed a train crossing the road.

"He must have been talking or laughing, but he did notice quick enough to swerve and miss the train,"

“They [BYU] wanted somebody with experience running the single wing, and I was the only Mormon around still using it.”

– LaVell Edwards

Philo said. “He ran off the road and hit into the crossing sign, damaging the car.”

LaVell did have the car repaired before his father came home.

Postscript to that story: LaVell later taught driver's education at Granite High.

At Utah State, LaVell Edwards was a star. People don't realize, say his friends, how good an athlete he really was.

San Francisco dentist De Van Robins was a teammate of LaVell's at USU and still drills the Edwards family's teeth.

“LaVell played center and linebacker and got to be team captain,” Robins said. “He wasn't elected. It wasn't a democracy under coach [John] Roning. But LaVell was a leader.”

Robins remembers when LaVell actually played quarterback for Roning.

Right, quarterback.

Roning came out in a single wing and picked LaVell, a linebacker, as quarterback—though actually he was a blocker. USU played Arizona State with the alignment, with LaVell in the lineup, the Aggies drove the length of the field and scored.

Robins claims Edwards hasn't changed his personality one iota from those days.

“He was never one to be cocky and was always down to earth,” Robins said. “That's just LaVell, the way he was then and the way he is now.”

Robins remembers one USU assistant coach whose personality clashed with LaVell's—as hard as that might be to imagine.

“This coach was on him like a rooster on a June bug,” Robins said.

“Now, LaVell hated to run. Any distance. And one day after practice we were asked to run wind sprints and do laps.

“After several laps the coach signaled for me to stop and shower, but told LaVell to keep going. I showered. I saw the coach come in and shower. I

asked everyone if they had seen LaVell. They hadn't. I looked for LaVell, but he wasn't in the shower or the locker room.

"I went outside and there in the dusk, across the field, was the shadow of LaVell. He was still running. The coach entirely forgot about him, and he wouldn't quit.

"And he never grumbled a bit."

> "He's just genuinely honest, and doing the right thing the right way is very important to him."
>
> —Patti LaVell

Dick Felt, a longtime BYU assistant, remains close to LaVell. Felt first met his former boss when Felt was a high school senior at Lehi, Utah State's Roning brought Aggie captain Edwards down on a recruiting trip.

"I was impressed," said Felt, who now jokes with Edwards about that day, "but not impressed enough to go to Utah State."

Working through two decades with Edwards, Felt now is even more impressed.

"The way he handles young men is outstanding," Felt said. "He's honest and patient with players, and genuinely likes these young men. He teaches that there's more to life than football and that, in my opinion, separates him from other college coaches.

"His players respect him. You see that after years, when they return. You don't acquire that respect just by being a coach, you have to earn it."

Robins believes Edwards has created proper priorities in his life and refuses to let anything infringe or change them.

"His God and family are that core and nothing disturbs it," Robins said. "He has that ability to understand that what is really significant is what counts. The other doesn't intrude. If he had lost the Holiday Bowl [in 1984], he wouldn't have let it intrude in his core."

Almost everyone agrees that, though his personality doesn't seem to be the right fit at first blush, LaVell definitely wound up in the right profession.

Though Edwards grew up a fruit farmer, sold shoes in a Salt Lake City Sears store, worked for city recreation departments and taught physical education, friends and family agree that he was born to coach.

"It's hard to imagine him not being a football coach. He always wanted to be one. He never had any other aspirations that I know of," Robins said.

"He got involved in physical educa-

tion to become a coach. But later in life, he turned to the intellectual part and earned his doctorate. I believe he could do anything he wanted in life.

"I don't know if he is the best X-and-O coach. But his great value is his ability to work with a person one-on-one and motivate. They may find a coach to replace him, but they cannot replace the man. People tell me he isn't a disciplinarian like Bo Schembechler, but I think he is. He's probably one of the greatest that ever lived.

"He's like one of those parents who don't have to shout at children to make them obey. He just sits and quietly asks them to do something. And it gets done."

By all accounts, this is a special man.

In 1984, the day before the final regular-season coaches poll came out, LaVell and his wife, Patti, were en route to the airport and New York City. LaVell had yet to cast his final ballot.

A little miffed after reports from around the country indicated that some voters deliberately left BYU out of the rankings so members of certain conferences would fare better, Patti asked her husband to leave Oklahoma out of the Top 20 when he voted.

Remember now, in that year of

One thing has been consistent with LaVell Edwards . . . he's always been a winner.

controversy, Sooner coach Barry Switzer had publicly ridiculed BYU's conference and schedule.

"When I said that, he just kind of looked at me and didn't say anything." Patti recalled.

LaVell went to a telephone and called his votes.

When he returned, Patti asked: "Where did you vote Oklahoma?"

"I voted them number three," LaVell said.

So much for retribution.

The only time her husband gets upset at home, Patti claims, is when a family member becomes less than what he or she should be.

"Like me getting caustic about Barry Switzer," Patti said. "He's just genuinely honest, and doing the right thing the right way is very important to him."

LaVell is the answer to an amazing question.

Can an unselfish fruit-picker who loves God, his family and Willie Nelson, who coached the single wing but practically re-invented the forward pass, actually win a national championship and become one of the greatest coaches in college football history?

By now, everyone knows the answer.

BYU
BYU

Bud

the HOLIDAY BOWL
23 KFMB

CHAPTER

FIVE

The most athletic and probably the most exciting of BYU's quarterback heroes was future Super Bowl winner Steve Young.

5

One If

“As far as complexity and sophistication, BYU’s offense is every bit as tough as any in the NFL.”

– Ty Detmer
Quarterback
Philadelphia Eagles

By Air

IT HAPPENS under a hot August sun, during two-a-days drills.

The BYU passing machine first sputters, then flares into ignition.

Quarterbacks line up behind centers, take snaps, make reads, throw passes, then report what they saw and how they made their decisions on where to throw.

Receivers race off the line of scrimmage, memorizing formations and how adjustments to those formations are supposed to be made according to how a defense reacts.

Running backs and tight ends take off at the snap count, too, either joining the passing routes, moving into a blocking position or filling a hole in a defensive seam—again, all according to reads and adjustments.

Bodies are spread everywhere. Balls are in the air. Coaches are pointing to areas on the field, then to defensive players, then to the spacing on the field.

An entire set of pre-snap reads already has been drilled into offensive players against man-to-man coverage. Another set is required for zones.

When a mixture of zone and man defenses are deployed, quarterbacks and receivers must recognize switches and change their routes accordingly.

Offensive linemen have reads and calls to learn, as well. The center hollers out certain blocking schemes as he checks linebackers, defensive linemen and formations.

Assembling the Cougar passing game is something like putting together pieces of an orchestra, then waiting for the music.

The BYU passing game has been known throughout college football, but perhaps its most dramatic impact on the game came when Robbie Bosco led the Cougars to a national championship in 1984.

And just as in the case of the guys who pitch and catch the ball, once more there's a good possibility that the pre-snap read can change, requiring one lineman to shift and help another, or perhaps a running back will have to plug a hole.

It all looks like controlled chaos.

BYU coaches insist it's really much simpler than people think.

There is no dispute, however, that assembling the Cougar passing game is something like putting together pieces of an orchestra, then waiting for the music.

For the last two decades, more or less, the tune has sounded just fine.

The oft-studied, occasionally imitated BYU attack hasn't changed much over the years. But then, back in the mid-1970s, it seemed almost light years ahead of other college offenses.

In the early days, defenders were so confused that the Cougars sometimes looked like they were playing 11 men against, oh, seven or eight.

When executed properly, BYU's passing game almost assures that a receiver will be open, somewhere, in the time necessary for unloading the football.

Of course, that sounds wonderful, but quarterbacks and receivers all have to make those magical adjustments, on time, for passes to be away and winging before the play blows up.

Which is why that August repetition and all those countless explanations are necessary. To play offense at BYU, you not only have to know how a route is run, but why.

"As far as complexity and sophistication, BYU's offense is every bit as tough as any in the NFL," Philadephia Eagle quarterback Ty Detmer said.

Listen to former Dallas Cowboy personnel guru Gil Brandt: "BYU has as good an offensive concept as anyone—college or pro—in football."

LaVell Edwards, the man credited with constructing this monster, admits he did because his Cougars were undermanned in the early '70s by bigger and faster opponents.

LaVell Edwards was smart to attract some of the best architects of the passing game onto his staff at BYU, including Doug Scovil (right) and future Green Bay head coach Mike Holmgren.

When Edwards got the BYU job, he wanted to do something different. He noted how successful BYU was in throwing the football when Virgil Carter bombarded defenses under former coach Tommy Hudspeth.

One of Edwards' hires was a guy named Dewey Warren, a former quarterback at Tennessee who loved throwing the ball. The Cougars weren't trying to revolutionize football at the time, just hoping to add enough of a passing game to put defenses in different situations. In his first season as head coach, Edwards had a big, strong, blonde-haired running back name Pete Van Valkenburg. He was hard to tackle and routinely hammered his way to first downs.

Edwards kept going to the well and Van Valkenburg ended up winning the NCAA rushing title in 1972.

But the Cougar staff was expanding its horizons. Edwards received approval to add a couple of coaches, and a few seasons later, he added a ninth coach, a graduate assistant named Norm Chow.

Perhaps the most dramatic catalyst for improvement was the hiring of another assistant, Doug Scovil, who had worked with passing game innovator Sid Luckman and other coaches in California.

Scovil, who had a knack for creativity, brought an air of confidence to BYU's offense, a touch Edwards liked. Scovil also make some X-and-O adjustments to the passing game, combining ideas already in place with some ideas from elsewhere.

And by now, Edwards and the Cougars were committed to throwing the ball.

Then throwing it some more.

BYU had gratifying early success with quarterback Gary Shiede, but the passing assault truly took off under the whip of a Provo native, Gifford Nielsen.

The Cougars dazzled opponents by utilizing the tight end, the running backs—even misdirection routes—and all those on-the-fly reads, and sometimes BYU actually appeared unstoppable.

"In those early days, it was like taking candy from a baby," Edwards said.

Through the years that followed, a ton of fine-tuning took place and when Scovil left, Edwards replaced him with Wally English, who liked a lot of motion and the old stand-up shift of the Dallas Cowboys.

English's theories never caught on and Edwards hired Ted Tollner, who was followed by Mike Holmgren, and finally Chow.

All of these assistants were given free rein to experiment and each polished the execution and added some new weapons to the arsenal.

It's pretty obvious that, among his other talents, Edwards had a knack for selecting talented assistants. Scovil ended up coaching with the Chicago

"THAT IS THE ESSENCE OF THE BYU QUARTERBACK: THE ABILITY TO INSTANTLY MAKE THE RIGHT DECISON AND GO WITH IT."

– NORM CHOW

Back in the early 1970s, Gary Shiede was the first BYU quarterback to be turned loose with the college game's most sophisticated passing attack.

The Cougar aerial assault has produced All Americans on the receiving end of all those throws, too, including star tight end Gordon Hudson in the early 1980s.

Bears before taking the head coaching job at San Diego State.

Tollner became head coach at Southern California, then San Diego State. Holmgren led the Green Bay Packers to a 1997 Super Bowl championship after coaching Joe Montana and Steve Young as the quarterback coach—and then offensive coordinator—of the San Francisco 49ers.

"Scovil really put some fire into this offense," said Chow, who has studied, worked and taught BYU's philosophy longer than anyone except Edwards.

"We have eight basic routes. That's the BYU passing game—eight simple plays. You come in as a freshman, you learn the offense in two days.

"Then you spend two years learning how to run it. We will disguise each of those routes with a variety of formations. We can run the same play at you four times and you don't recognize it until the receiver has the ball.

"That drill we run in practice—every time the quarterback throws the ball, he has to come and tell me why—what he saw, what he was thinking. By the time we hand you the keys, you know the offense and how to read what you see on the field.

"Where is the second receiver? Where is the third?

"That is the essence of the BYU quarterback: the ability to instantly make the right decison and go with it."

In a newspaper interview during BYU's 14–1 season in 1996, assistant coach Robbie Bosco—the guy who led the Cougars to a perfect 13–0 season in 1984—recalled the first time he saw BYU's offense as a teen watching TV in northern California.

"Up until then, I really hadn't given BYU much thought. But what I saw that day just mesmerized me. The quarterback then was Marc Wilson, and the first four balls he threw went for touchdowns. It was incredible. The game was a rout with five minutes left in the first quarter. I had never seen anything like it."

Half a decade later, after paying his dues in the system, Bosco was throttling Michigan in the Holiday Bowl in San Diego, helping win a national championship.

"This is a simple offense, really,"

The quarterback list is full of heroes, including former Provo High legend Gifford Neilsen.

It's hard to imagine any school in the past two decades has prepared more quarterbacks for the NFL—including future pro Marc Wilson.

Jim McMahon may have been a rebel compared to the rest of BYU's star quarterbacks, but he produced bushels of touchdowns and earned the reputation of being a guy who could always find a way to win.

BYU

Bosco said, echoing the gospel according to Norm Chow. "Just attack the defense, make it commit itself, then pick it apart."

Over the years, BYU quarterbacks and coaches have seen every imaginable defensive ploy thrown at them—everything but the kitchen sink. Teams have tried one-man pass rushes in front of a 10-man zone, and nine-man defensive fronts that lead to all-out blitzes.

Chow remembers running into a coaching friend who had just quit as an assistant at UTEP, and he showed Chow the book he had kept on BYU. "It looked like the Encyclopedia Britannica," Chow said.

Another weekend, Chow picked up a newspaper in Fort Collins, Colo., and saw some of BYU's plays diagrammed out on the front page.

Cougars coaches laugh at that sort of thing. They aren't hiding anything. But knowing the BYU offense and stopping it aren't exactly the same thing.

"The key to our offense," Chow said, "is repetition and the fact we have never lost confidence in it. In all these years, we have never wavered. You can beat us 50–0 and next week we'll be back running this offense and doing the same thing.

"And the man who really deserves the credit is LaVell Edwards. He likes to tell people he doesn't understand the offense—but he's the one who put it in here, 25 years ago when nobody thought it would work. He's the one who had the courage to stick with it, no matter what."

In a quarter-century as head coach at BYU, Edwards has seen all kinds of quarterbacks—tall and short, strong-armed or merely accurate, gifted runners and pocket passers—master his offense and bust NCAA records.

Likewise, Edwards never has wavered from his formula of being loyal to his assistants and players. As a result, he has watched this offense—once considered a gimmick—open the door to victories over Miami, Notre Dame, Michigan, Penn State, UCLA, Washington, Colorado and Texas A&M.

A school that once could not compete suddenly became a national power, consistently ranked among the elite in college football.

But one of the more amazing aspects of the Edwards air show has been his staff's ability to churn out record-breaking quarterbacks.

Nielsen earned All-America honors while leading the nation in passing and contending for the Heisman Trophy in 1977, the season Earl Campbell of Texas won it.

Marc Wilson took over for Nielsen and passed for a WAC-record seven touchdowns at Colorado State in his first game.

Jim McMahon, who shared time with Wilson and ultimately replaced him, tied or broke more than 60 NCAA records, not to mention leading BYU to its first-ever bowl victory, the "Hail Mary" comeback against SMU in 1980.

Steve Young became the most accurate passer in NCAA history, replacing McMahon when many thought it could never be done.

Robbie Bosco not only has the distinction of passing the Cougars to an undefeated season, but doing it in his first year at the helm.

The national championship QB in '84 (inset), Bosco learned the BYU offense well enough to become LaVell Edwards' quarterback coach.

Gifford Neilsen was the guy who helped take the BYU passing game from something of a novelty to the nationally known weapon it has become.

Then came Bosco, a fourth All-American quarterback in Provo, and that 1984 performance that led to a national title.

How successful were these guys?

From 1979 through '85—riding on the wings of McMahon, Young and Bosco—the Cougars were 60–9.

Then a few years later, long after many BYU fans thought they'd seen it all, a Texan named Ty Detmer came along and seemed to have mastered BYU's offense almost the day he walked on campus.

Elected team captain as a sophomore, Detmer won the Heisman Trophy as a junior. Overall, he threw for a whopping 15,031 yards at BYU—well over 5,000 more than McMahon, who ranks second on the Cougars' glittering career list.

John Walsh added his name to list in the early 1990s, then gave up his senior year for the NFL draft, forcing BYU to dip into the junior college ranks, where they found a diamond in 1995.

Steve Sarkisian, a transfer from El Camino College in California, took the reins without the usual BYU prep courses. Sark started in spring practice in '95, and while still learning on the job, set an NCAA record his first year by completing 92 percent of his passes against Fresno State.

Even some lesser-known quarterbacks learned to function smoothly in the BYU offense, players like Blaine Fowler (left) and Ryan Hancock. Fowler contributed some critical minutes for the Cougars as Robbie Bosco's backup in the 1984 national championship season.

Sarkisian helped BYU win a WAC championship his first season, and of course, he was the trigger man for the joyous 14–1 stampede of 1996—winning the NCAA passing title almost a matter of course.

So what else is new?

Five of the top 11 single-season passing efficiency performances in NCAA history belong to BYU quarterbacks—two by Detmer and one each by Sarkisian, McMahon and Young.

Edwards refuses to compare his quarterbacks. But they have been as different in personality as they've been in physical skills and delivery.

Nielsen probably was the most positive-minded, public relations-oriented of them all. After his great season, he was drafted by the Oilers and eventually used his communication skills to become sports director for KHOU-TV in Houston.

Wilson, the tallest at 6-foot-6, was the quietest but had one of the strongest arms. He was drafted by the Los Angles Raiders, where he started for a few years.

McMahon, the most controversial, had the quickest release, best pocket awareness and could read defenses among the best. Jimmy Mac never watched film, but he had a natural ability to understand schemes on defense and offense.

McMahon was a spectacular winner as a pro—on and off the field. After leading the Chicago Bears to the 1985 Super Bowl, he played with Minnesota, Phoenix, Philadelphia and the Packers.

Young was probably the most insecure, but driven and charismatic, and easily the best overall athlete of the group. Pro scouts always have contended that Young, who is headed to the NFL Hall of Fame, could have had a great career as a running back.

Bosco, a gutty strong-armed thrower, was quiet like Wilson. Bosco was drafted by the Packers but never enjoyed an NFL career because of a shoulder injury.

Detmer, whose Heisman Trophy in 1990 might have come—at least in part—because of all those outstanding

Cougar fans like to argue about which of their quarterbacks had the best arm, but it might have been John Walsh.

Offensive coordinator Norm Chow, who has been on the Cougar staff more than two decades, gets coaching offers from other schools routinely but he's stayed at BYU to rev up another passing juggernaut.

In 1995, Steve Sarkisian became the first junior college transfer to inherit the BYU quarterback job. A year later, Sark led the nation in passing and guided the Cougars to 14 wins and a No. 5 national ranking.

performances before him, could be the most popular of all the QBs among BYU fans.

Ty's southern accent, general affability, one-of-the-guys personality and competitive spirit somehow caught the fancy of Cougar partisans for whom touchdown passes were nothing new.

Except for arm strength (Ty is no fireballer), Detmer and McMahon are comparable in their accuracy and play-making. With 121 career touchdowns and that bushel basket of passing yards, Detmer made the most of more playing time than his predecessors.

Ironically, even though he wound up as one of the most prolific college passers of all time, Detmer was not chosen until the ninth round of the NFL draft.

Edwards thought that was a mistake, and said so at the time.

"When he gets his chance, Ty will play well as a pro," Edwards insisted. "The right situation will come up, and he'll take advantage of it."

As usual, LaVell was right.

After backing up Packers superstar Brett Farve through the '95 season, Detmer signed as a free agent with Philadelphia and won his first starting job in 1996.

Sarkisian, who was only about 6-feet-and-change and couldn't quite throw rockets, was not drafted by the NFL at all (Edwards sniffs at that slight, too . . .), but signed to play in the Canadian Football League.

Along with Young, Sarkisian may have been one of the most outgoing, quotable Cougars, and he shared that ability to find victories with guys like McMahon and Bosco.

They've been an amazing group, the BYU quarterbacks. The system that produced them is pretty special, too.

And simple.

At least according to the coaches.

By far the most prolific BYU quarterback in terms of statistics, Texas-born Ty Detmer also became the school's first Heisman Trophy winner.

CHAPTER

SIX

An enthusiastic crowd of fans is always behind the BYU Cougars and over the years they've witnessed some of the greatest games in college football history.

6

The Greatest

Games

HOW DO YOU EVEN START trying to choose the best games in BYU history?

There's been so much drama, so much history.

But excluding the two miracle seasons—1984 and 1996, plus their penultimate bowl victories—it really is possible to narrow the list of satisfying heart-stoppers.

To three.

Of course every Cougar fan is entitled to his or her own favorite—for instance, just about any win over Utah belongs on the highlight reel—but just to cut all the arguments off sometime before the millenium, here's the trio of triumphs that top the chart:

1. December 12, 1980 — BYU 46, SMU 45 in the Holiday Bowl
2. October 15, 1994 — BYU 21, Notre Dame 14 at South Bend, Indiana
3. September 8, 1990 — BYU 28, Miami 21 at Provo

Sure, there have plenty more wins, and even some losses, that qualify as bona fide memory-makers. But the top three all boast a particular spice, something a little bit beyond mere success or failure, which sets them apart.

The bowl win over SMU was BYU's first-ever postseason victory, and it finished with perhaps the most famous single play in school history.

Enough said.

Gutty Jim McMahon urged his teammates not to give up when SMU raced away to a huge lead in the Holiday Bowl, sparking the most remarkable comeback ever for BYU.

The conquest of Notre Dame—on the road, under the shadow of the Golden Dome, no less—perhaps says as much about the opponent as it does of the Cougars. Notre Dame, after all, is Notre Dame.

Does the Gipper ring a bell? How about Knute Rockne?

And maybe the same thing is true of that shocking upset of No. 1-ranked Miami, only in an opposite sense. Somehow, the 'Canes of the late 1980s and early '90s came to represent outlaw talent. In the shadow of the Wasatch Mountains, they were brash, bold, brazen—and beaten.

So even if there are other games which tickle your particular fancy, it's impossible to dispute that those three triumphs belong in the scrapbook.

The "Hail Mary" Bowl

This one was so dramatic that 15 years after the 1980 Holiday Bowl, a panel of sports writers voted BYU's miracle comeback victory over Southern Methodist as one of the most thrilling college football games of all time.

The matchup featured some big names. And a fourth quarter that would be hard to imagine by Hollywood scriptwriters.

Jim McMahon, who would later lead Mike Ditka's Chicago Bears to the 1985 Super Bowl, was the Cougar quarterback. SMU's offense, meanwhile, was powered by two of the best running backs in Southwest Conference history—Eric Dickerson and Craig James.

Dickerson went on to become the NFL's leading rusher in a magnificent career with the Rams and Colts. James was a decent pro, too, but he became even better-known as a popular TV analyst.

SMU dominated the Cougars through most of three quarters that night, which helped set the stage for a final period that still is unmatched in school history.

The events of the final 15 minutes were so bizarre that many Cougar fans at the game actually left Jack Murphy Stadium and drove clear home to Utah, only to find out the next day that BYU had won.

Setting the stage: McMahon had tuned up for his first bowl start by leading the Cougars to 56–6 and 54–16 bombings of Utah and UNLV.

After a season-opening upset loss at New Mexico, the Cougars won 11 straight games and were as potent offensively as any team in the land.

BYU averaged 49 points per game in 1980 and tossed for more than 400 yards whenever offensive coordinator Doug Scovil could sneak some of those stats past LaVell Edwards at the end of lopsided victories.

McMahon set 34 NCAA records and threw for 4,571 yards. His season passing efficiency mark of 176.6 broke a 14-year old record held by Jerry Rhome of Tulsa. McMahon's mark ultimately stood for more than a decade.

BYU was ranked 15th and the Mustangs No. 19 entering the Holiday Bowl, which was only in its third year of existence and looking any kind of national exposure.

Not only did SMU feature the explosive sophomores James and Dickerson, the Ponies also had Michael Carter, a defensive lineman who would win an Olympic medal in the shot put and play on some great 49ers teams.

And for three quarters, SMU put on a show. The Cougars were pushed around, run over and thoroughly whipped.

SMU just lined up and played smash-mouth football, making Edwards' team look like a bunch of pop-gun sissies from the no-account WAC.

Through the third quarter, James had rushed for a whopping 225 yards and on the other side of the ball, Carter had hounded McMahon relentlessly, sacking him twice.

Needless to say, Jimmy Mac was not taking this public humiliation lightly. He hated to lose at anything, let alone be booted all over the field on national TV.

As the game went along, it appeared that BYU's 11–1 record not only was a fraud, but McMahon's All-America citation a joke.

When James broke loose for another touchdown in the fourth quarter, SMU led the Cougars 45–25 and coach Ron Meyer began substituting liberally.

On the sidelines, TV cameras showed the SMU players laughing, slapping hands and pointing at the crowd and mouthing phrases like, "Hi, Mom."

Across the way, BYU's bench looked like death on a skillet. Players and coaches were trying to maintain

Oblivious to the momentous events to come, BYU players went to San Diego to enjoy themselves first and face talented SMU in the Holiday Bowl afterward. Calvin Close made friends with a dolphin at Sea World, while Waymon Hamilton and Eric Lane made sure their trip to California was a good ol' time.

Perhaps the most famous play in BYU history, the "Hail Mary" throw to win the 1980 Holiday Day: Somehwere in a tangle of fallen SMU defenders, Cougar tight end Clay Brown is clutching the football after hauling in a last-second, desperation TD heave from quarterback Jim McMahon.

So it was down to one play, three seconds on the clock, 41 yards from heaven. There was nothing for Scovil to do but call for the "Hail Mary" pass.

the bearing of a WAC champion, but it was a major task for anyone to keep his eyes off the ground.

McMahon was livid. While many fans at home were turning off their TV sets and the Cougar faithful in the stands had seen enough, the feisty quarterback was trying to set a fire under his teammates.

The miracle started with 3:58 remaining in the game.

With BYU stalled near midfield and facing a fourth down, the coaching staff motioned for a punt.

"Are we giving up?" McMahon yelled. "Are we going to quit?"

McMahon refused to leave the field or allow the offensive players to switch with punt formation specialists. After a timeout, BYU came back out with its regular unit and McMahon tossed a pass to tight end Clay Brown for a first down.

The Cougars wound up marching 72 yards on that drive—taking about two and half minutes—and wrapped the thing up on a 15-yard TD pass from McMahon to Matt Braga.

When a two-point conversion attempt failed. BYU trailed 45–31.

The Cougars then tried what everybody knew they would, an onsides kick. And got it, when linebacker Todd Shell fell on the ball.

By this time, the Ponies were starting to get a little weary, and BYU took just four plays to set up Scott Phillips for a 1-yard dive into the end zone.

McMahon hit Phillips with a swing pass for a two-point conversion and the Cougars improbably had closed to 45–39.

No one on the SMU side was smiling or mugging for the cameras any longer.

The law of averages took over on BYU's second attempt at an onside kick. It failed. SMU took possession at midfield, needing only a single first down to run out the clock.

But momentum is a funny thing. SMU had been able to run almost at will earlier in the game, but with that big lead, the Mustangs had substituted—and relaxed.

Now they needed momentum back, and couldn't get it.

The series came down to a critical third-down play, with Dickerson desperately lunging for sideline marker on a sweep. But linebacker Glen Redd and corner Bill Schoeflin had other ideas, and Dickerson crashed down short.

SMU had to punt, but still, they had used up almost every precious second. On fourth down, the Mustangs allowed the 25-second play clock to expire with 18 seconds remaining.

The Mustangs reloaded and lined up to punt again, but Schoeflin, a pint-sized cornerback, shot around the SMU blockers and made a clean block.

The dream was still alive.

But the Cougars, who took over at the SMU 41, had just 13 seconds and they used 10 ticks as McMahon threw incomplete toward Brown and missed connections with speedster Lloyd Jones down the right sidelines.

So it was down to one play, three seconds on the clock, 41 yards from heaven. There was nothing for Scovil to do but call for the "Hail Mary" pass.

Down to business: Linebacker Glen Redd and the BYU defense rose up late to stuff a Southern Methodist team featuring future pro running backs Craig James and Eric Dickerson and set the stage for a dramatic victory.

The Cougars went wild after the "Hail Mary" pass that gave them a comeback for the ages and BYU's first-ever bowl victory.

BYU used a formation that called for the wide receivers to take off down the sidelines, while the backs hesitating a count before releasing, hoping to keep some linebackers occupied.

Brown ran a post pattern down the middle.

McMahon took the snap and hustled back. He waited, waited, waited—then took a few steps forward, buying time for Brown to run half the length of the field.

Finally, McMahon just threw the ball as hard as he could.

Brown found himself surrounded by Mustang defenders, but at 6-foot-4, he had a few inches on the defensive backs around him. Brown also had good timing. And super hands.

The ball came floating down out of the misty San Diego sky as six players converged in the middle of the end zone.

Bodies went up. Bodies came down.

And Brown had the football.

As the officials raised their hands to signal a touchdown, receiver Danny Plater went nuts, celebrating behind the pileup. And why not, since the Cougars had tied SMU by scoring 21 points in just over three minutes?

How kicker Kurt Gunther ever walked onto the field without tripping over his shaking legs is still a mystery.

But Gunther did make it in position to aim the PAT. With no time on the clock, his kick split the uprights.

Final: BYU 46–45.

That Holiday Bowl still is called the "Miracle Bowl," and for good reason.

When the Cougars went to historic Notre Dame Stadium, they were facing more than the ghosts of Knute Rockne and George Gipp. They'd been pounded by the Irish in the only two previous meetings between the schools.

Sorry, Gipper

BYU's victory over Notre Dame at South Bend in 1994 clearly was one of the more satisfying in Cougar history.

Sure, the Irish were a little down and coming off a loss. A couple of key running backs had been hurt. But it was Notre Dame.

And it was BYU, and however hard Cougar fans tried to supress, forget or ignore the obvious: It was Catholics versus the Mormons.

But never mind all that. Just playing Notre Dame is the complete experience, win or lose. Like 'em or not, the Irish are a force unto themselves in American college football. This is the school they write songs and make movies about.

Notre Dame has everything: history, the Four Horsemen, money from huge TV exposure, the Victory March, great players from anywhere the Irish choose to recruit, those famous golden helmets.

There's nothing like Notre Dame.

The week BYU played at South Bend in '94, the Fighting Irish had a 4–2 record. Their annual dream of being No. 1 was gone. What remained of the season after six games was the task of salvaging at least a respectable Notre Dame season and regaining some respect.

After an embarrassing 30–11 upset loss to Boston College the previous

BYU startled everyone by fighting the Irish on even terms and moving the ball well, as Jamal Willis gained yardage on a sweep.

Saturday, Notre Dame was smarting. So were the Irish's millions of fans, and they were pretty vocal about things.

The mighty house must be put back in order.

The players were listening, and seemed equally motivated. "We will not have back-to-back losses," Irish quarterback Ron Powlus said.

Oh, and for all of Notre Dame's supposed problems that year, the Irish were a 16-point favorite. The Cougars were 5–1, but they'd lost to Colorado

Surprisingly, the BYU defense held its own against Notre Dame's huge and potent offensive line. John Raass' battle with the beefy Irish typified the Cougar effort.

BYU forced the generally unflappable Irish into several mistakes. Safety Eddie Sampson celebrated the recovery of a Notre Dame fumble.

State at home, beaten Hawaii by a single point, New Mexico and Fresno State each by two.

Not only did the Cougars appear to be something less than juggernaut, but their first two meetings with Notre Dame, in 1992 and '93, both had turned into disappointing blowouts.

The Irish cruised 42–16 at home in '92, then made their long-awaited first appearance in Provo the next season and physically punished BYU in a 45–20 romp.

And of all things, BYU's offense was struggling at that point in the 1994 season. Through six games, quarterback John Walsh had not played anywhere near the level he'd shown the previous season, when he nearly led the Cougars to a last-second upset of Ohio State in the Holiday Bowl.

Like Notre Dame, BYU had some legitimate excuses. September injuries to seniors Tim Nowatzke (ankle) and Bryce Doman (knee) left Walsh with some novice receivers who were lining up in the wrong places and running inconsistent routes.

Still, Walsh had the gun to shoot down anyone.

"John's best games are still ahead of him," Doman said prior to the Notre

Quarterback John Walsh, who'd been suffering through a mediocre season, had a great game at Notre Dame and then enjoyed the triumph with his parents.

The Irish, who had thumped BYU in Provo the previous season, had to be shocked at the Cougar defense. Notre Dame quarterback Ron Powlus, being sacked by Travis Hall, never had time to get comfortable.

Dame game. "He'll be the first to admit it. But we all know that because his best is ahead of him, we can only play better than we have."

Yet Notre Dame seemed an unlikely place for a turnaround. Since 1989, the Cougars had been pretty tame away from Provo. They hadn't won a non-conference road game in four and a half years—losing to Oregon State, UCLA (twice), Notre Dame and Penn State in that slump.

Once the Cougars arrived in South Bend, LaVell Edwards did something that most college coaches would consider almost suicidal: He decided his athletes should take a tour of the Notre Dame campus.

Edwards has always believed players should learn something from road trips—when in Philadelphia, see the Liberty Bell—but one would suspect gawking at Notre Dame history might be the all-time psych job.

In reverse.

But as usual, LaVell knew more than anyone else.

The Cougars not only weren't awed to the point of paralysis, they actually became motivated enough to play the Irish helmet to helmet, pad to pad.

BYU's only chance to compete with Notre Dame was to get physical at the line of scrimmage against one of the country's most bruising teams—but the Cougars did it.

In fact, BYU's sweet 21–14 victory over the 17th-ranked Irish was a case of the Cougars beating Lou Holtz's monsters at their own game, pounding away inside on the running of Jamal Willis and administering some serious licks on defense.

David Lauder kicked the two longest field goals of his career—49 and 48 yards— and Willis scored touchdowns on a 19-yard pass and 2-yard dive to setup the victory.

Walsh connected on 17 of 31 passes for 216 yards with one touchdown and an interception, but the important thing was that he stayed composed and hit several big throws when BYU had to have them.

BYU's defense continually slammed the gate on the Irish, who could not take advantage of the Cougars' beat-up secondary.

The Cougars turned the game around by stuffing Notre Dame after the Irish had chewed up 20 plays and gotten themselves into a first-and-goal situation from the BYU 3-yard line. John Pollock sacked Powlus for an 11-yard loss and the Irish missed a field goal.

There were other big defensive plays, too.

Greg Pitts recovered a fumble, linebacker Shay Muirbrook picked off a pass and Chad Lewis blocked his second field goal of the year.

"We got beat by a team that controlled the line of scrimmage and protected the passer better than we did," Holtz admitted afterward.

As the game clock wound down, BYU players, coaches and fans realized they were experiencing some college football magic. They were winning at Notre Dame, the home of

Finally: LaVell Edwards is congratuled by Notre Dame coach Lou Holtz after BYU added a giant notch to its football belt.

Rockne, Lujack, Theismann and Montana.

At Notre Dame!

Linebacker Stan Raass turned a cartwheel on the turf and guard Evan Pilgrim lifted Nowatzke into the air. Proud Notre Dame fans, tens of thousands in the stands and millions who watched on national television, sat stunned and shocked.

A band of 2,000-plus Cougar boosters who made the trek to that pigskin mecca screamed until their lungs burned.

"It's like a nightmare," Notre Dame defensive coordinator Bob Davie said. "It's devastating. There is no way to hide that. This is a devastating loss."

The Cougars were jubilant, but professed something less than shock.

"We knew last week we'd beat these guys," said Nowatzke, a product of nearby Michigan City, Indiana, who grew up wanting to play at Notre Dame. "We made up our minds early in the week we weren't playing the Four Horsemen, we weren't playing Joe Montana, we were playing a team we could beat, and we did not doubt it."

On a historic afternoon of football, it was there on the scoreboard.

No one could doubt it.

Facing one of the most potent offenses in college football, BYU and linebacker Shad Hansen (50) stood up to be counted on a wild night in Provo.

The "Ty-sman Trophy"

To win a Heisman Trophy, you need media exposure, publicity, a good marketing campaign and at least one huge game—on national TV—that rings the voters' chimes.

A Heisman candidate also has to get lucky.

It doesn't hurt, of course, if he plays for Notre Dame, Southern California or one of the Florida schools—like Miami. It helps if the talking heads on SportsCenter like you.

And naturally, a Heisman Trophy aspirant better be a heck of a player.

Like Ty Detmer.

As many yards as BYU's Texas-born quarterback amassed, however, he needed that strange and special confluence of events to snag Heisman votes, and then actually win the award.

That's exactly what happened during Detmer's junior year, 1990, when the Cougars played a September game at home against defending national champion Miami, which once again was ranked No. 1.

ESPN took a look at the BYU-Miami game and loved it immediately. The hype started even before season. Ironically, part of the attraction was early Heisman chatter, but it was directed mainly at Hurricane quarterback Craig Erickson.

Better yet for the cable network, Detmer definitely was in the Heisman hunt from the beginning—despite the obscurity of the Mountain Time Zone—because he'd had a monster soph season, throwing for 4,560 yards and 32 touchdowns.

Then there was the obvious Quarterback U. angle: Miami and BYU had great recent traditions at the position. The Cougars could boast of Detmer, Robbie Bosco, Steve Young, Jim McMahon, Marc Wilson and Gifford Nielsen, and Miami fans could roar back, "What about Erickson, George Mira, Jim Kelly, Bernie Kosar, Vinnie Testaverde, and Steve Walsh?"

Even before BYU's season opener at UTEP on Sept. 1, writers, fans and players were talking about Miami-BYU. It would be the biggest football game ever played in the state of Utah, by far.

No national champion had ever ventured into the state. Only the NCAA Final Four basketball tournament in Salt Lake City had attrracted more media. More than 300 press credentials were issued for the September 8 game in Provo.

A record crowd of 66,235 packed Cougar Stadium that night, making it the largest gathering for a sporting event in state history. Only the deer hunt could claim more interest – and that lasts for 11 days.

"Ty Detmer is one of the best quarterbacks in the country," Miami coach Dennis Erickson gushed. "He understands their offense very well. He's truly a great player. We hope to just slow him down a bit.

"Craig is a little bit bigger and very much the same player. He's smart and understands the game. The key is knowing where to go with the football. In that, [Detmer and Erickson] have very much in common."

LaVell Edwards was worried all summer.

"We face the best quarterbacks in the country," he told writers. "We open up against Howard Gasser, then Erickson. Then we host Washington State and Brad Gossen.

"We play Oregon's Bill Musgrave, who joined Detmer setting an NCAA record for passing in one game last year. We'll face Dan McGwire of San Diego State, who is rated as one of the best in the nation."

Edwards had other concerns, too.

Miami's defense was rated No. 1 in the country the previous season. It was one of the most dominating units Edwards had watched in all his years of coaching.

"I've never seen a better defensive line." Edwards said, matching Dennis Erickson compliment for compliment. "It may go down as the best in history. I saw the film of Miami against San Diego State last year, and that defense sacked McGuire 10 times and knocked him down at least half as many times again—and they never blitzed once."

Miami's most fearsome linemen from 1989 had been drafted the previous April—except Russell Maryland. And every preseason publication suggested that Maryland, an All-America tackle and almost unstoppable pass rusher, was a top candidate for the Outland Trophy.

Ty Detmer put himself in position to win the 1990 Heisman Trophy with a spectacular performance as BYU upset No.1-ranked Miami before a national television audience.

The hype seemed to flow by the hour, on both sides.

Edwards did have some legitimate fears, though. BYU could not emulate Miami's team speed in practice. The Canes could fly: Linebacker Jesse Armstead was faster than anyone on the BYU roster.

As America watched the drama unfold during game week, the underdog Cougars caught the attention of the country.

Could David slay Goliath?

Would Miami repeat as national champion?

Cougar receiver Matt Bellini was one of many targets for QB Ty Detmer as mighty Miami went down.

Was this guy Detmer for real?

And what about the Heisman?

Miami is not one of the most popular football teams in college football. At the 1987 Fiesta Bowl, Miami players insulted Joe Paterno and Penn State by showing up for a press conference dressed in green army fatigues. Hurricane players notorious for taunting opponents after big plays.

Some of the Canes' end-zone antics actually led to NCAA legislation banning demeaning behavior by players—the taunting rule. Eventually, Miami had a big hand in getting celebrations outlawed entirely.

Miami players were also known for talking trash on and off the field. Reporters could count on Miami football players for good copy. They didn't mind popping off and insulting someone, because they could back it up.

And so the BYU-Miami matchup got its share of pregame smack.

For instance, Hurricane defensive end Shane Curry on Detmer: "I don't think he's better than Craig or smarter than Steve Walsh. We face a guy like him every day. We plan on hitting him a lot. We want to be in his face a lot."

Quarterback Erickson was slightly more diplomatic than his teammates—but not much. "[Detmer] is a better golfer than I am," Erickson said. "That's about as far as I'll go."

On and on it went, as one Miami player after another questioned the Cougars' manhood, their apparent lack of speed, their weak schedule. Nonstop trash.

BYU's players took exception.

Offensive tackle Neal Fort said Miami was No. 1 and deserved respect, but no Miami player would be wearing an "S" on his chest and flying around with a cape.

"They aren't Supermen," Fort said. "They went to a high school just like everybody else. They're playing college football just like I am."

And as usual, Detmer put the whole conversation into perspective. "It seems BYU is always having to prove it can play with the big boys," he said.

End of talk.

Time to play.

September 8 was an unusually hot day in Provo. Even in the late afternoon, the temperature hovered around 90 degrees—call it Miami without the humidity.

Around the county, most serious college football fans scheduled their plans around the game. This was No. 1 Miami against No. 16 BYU, and the thing had a unique appeal, even if the Canes were 13½-point favorites.

Amazingly, ABC analyst (and Miami Dolphin Hall of Famer) Bob Griese went miles out on a limb and picked BYU to beat Miami.

Whoa.

But more in tune with public perception, CNN/USA Today oddsmaker Danny Sheridan chose Miami not only to win the game, but run off with another national championship.

Sheridan quipped, "BYU has about

as much chance of upsetting this team as the Vatican Swiss Guards would have of defeating the U.S. Marines. Cute uniforms, no ammunition. You get the picture."

BYU didn't install anything fancy into its offensive package for Miami, but offensive coordinator Roger French and quarterback coach Norm Chow did polish up a one-step dropback for Detmer to speed up his delivery.

With Maryland and Armstead on the other side of the line, the longer it took the play to get from snap to finish, the more chance Detmer would be in danger.

BYU did have one obvious advantage besides the home field. The Cougars had played UTEP a week earlier, and ironed out some kinks in a 30–10 victory. Miami, for all its talent, was coming in without a tune-up.

Just before the national anthem, a dozen Miami players lined up and pointed their index fingers into the air, displaying the familiar No. 1 sign. The group turned and pointed to the crowd, then to BYU's players on the south end of the stadium.

Talk about nerve.

But the Canes always seem to back up their rhetoric and, sure enough, they scored first on a 7-yard run by Stephen McGuire to lead 7–0.

Was this the beginning of the end?

Perhaps it should have been. BYU couldn't move the ball early in the game, and looked jittery most of the night. The Cougars fumbled five times and lost an interception, which against a team like Miami, is going to be fatal 99 times out of a hundred.

As the game wore on and Miami continued to struggle, Cougars defensive tackle Rich Kaufusi had reason to show his emotion.

Ah, but that one other time . . .

The Canes kept that 7–0 lead through a quarter, but something subtle was taking place. The BYU defense was holding its own.

When Miami speedsters McGuire and Leonard Conley ran wide out of the backfield, BYU linebackers Alema Fitsemanu and Jerod Leavitt would force the play out of bounds for little gain. Up front, Rich Kafusi, Mark Smith and Pete Harston were taking on All-America tackles Mike Sullivan and Luis Cristobal—without giving ground. When Miami failed to increase that first-quarter lead and stick the Cougars into a serious hole, the Hurricane offense started pressing. And then truly struggling.

The Miami pass rush punished Ty Detmer, who took a helmet under the chin at one point and had to be stitched up. Trainer T.J. Burne looked at the cut, which left Detmer with a scar for life.

Erickson continually overthrew receivers who were wide open. On the sidelines, his teammates started turning against him, complaining he was killing the team. Shouting, finger-pointing—the Canes weren't haven't too much fun.

BYU's offense finally kicked into gear on the first series of the second quarter, with Detmer leading the Cougars on a 60-yard, seven-play scoring drive. Matt Bellini caught a 14-yard touchdown pass in the corner of the end zone.

On the scoring play, Miami appeared to have BYU stopped. The defense flushed Detmer from the pocket, but Ty dodged linebacker Shane Curry and somehow stepped out of Maryland's grasp. Detmer eventually unloaded the TD pass while on the dead run, lofting it just over the hands of cornerback Ryan McNeil.

"He's one slimy cat," Bellini said of Detmer's escape.

Just five minutes later, Earl Kauffman booted a 32-yard field goal to put the Cougars up 10–7. You could almost sense the national TV audience edging closer to the screen.

This was a football game.

The Cougars coughed up a fumble on their next possession and Miami immediately made the most of it, pounding the ball from the BYU 43 to the 2-yard line. McGuire danced in from there, nearly untouched, putting Miami back up 14–10 with 1:42 left before intermission.

But Detmer and Co. didn't want anyone headed toward the refrigerator too early.

The Cougars struck back, as Detmer ripped Miami apart with seven straight strikes. Detmer made it look so easy, the Hurricanes were stunned.

BYU's receivers had shaken off early nerves and were working themselves into the seams of Miami's secondary, forcing the quicker Canes to cover every square inch of turf 40 yards from the line of scrimmage. It wasn't something Miami had to do very often.

Detmer drove BYU to the Miami 2-yard line, where he ignored heavy pressure and rifled a pass to Andy Boyce for a 17–14 lead.

Repairs were necessary at halftime. Detmer had caught a helmet under the chin following one wild Miami rush, and he had to be sewn up.

"I'll take six stitches for a good deep sideline pattern anytime," Detmer said afterward.

Meanwhile, Miami's trash-talker's had some re-thinking to do. The Canes had allowed just 270 yards total offense per game the previous year, but swallowed 332 yards from the Cougars in the first half. Executing a game plan that called for throwing underneath routes, Detmer completed passes for 200 yards in the second quarter alone. During the first half, a writer called his desk back in Florida from the press box and said, "I can't believe it. BYU's slow white guys are open all over the field."

But Miami, predictably, was far from done.

The second half opened with Erickson taking the Canes 80 yards, where Conley scored from the 7. And it looked pitifully easy.

No doubt a lot of BYU fans wondered at that moment if all the excitement and emotion of the first 30 minutes had left the Cougars exhausted and dead.

It seemed like a valid question, but the answer was no.

Kauffman capped a Cougar drive by drilling a 29-yard field goal to draw BYU within 21–20 with 9:26 remaining in the third quarter.

Barely a minute later, Miami's coach Erickson—sensing the need to keep scoring—gambled on fourth-and-one at the Canes' 44-yard line. This was a pivotal play, maybe the biggest of the game. If Miami picked up the first down, momentum almost surely would build and the Canes would be zooming into the end zone.

Even though it was still just the third quarter, everyone in the stadium sensed that the moment of truth was at hand.

On earlier short-yardage plays, McGuire had delivered two scoring runs with scant opposition. There was little reason to doubt he'd pick up the paltry one yard Miami needed.

But BYU had adrenalin left, and McGuire never made it past the line of scrimmage as Harston, Kaufusi and Beigel swarmed over him, then buried him in a pile.

BYU took possession at the Miami 43, and nine plays later, Detmer rocked the Hurricane defense with another pinpoint pass.

Denver Post columnist Dick Connor described the game-turning play in detail:

"One freeze frame should be blown up and left on the locker room wall. It will show Miami defenders Kipp Vickers, Shane Curry, Jessie Armstead and Eric Miller all stomach down.

"Meanwhile, seven yards away in the end zone, Mike Salido has the winning touchdown. And standing over the flattened quartet, Detmer is clapping his hands with glee.

"When the play started, Salido was a junior. By the time Detmer ran around, shed one tackler after another, waited for someone to come open and finally found Salido, he was a senior.

"Detmer pumped, pulled the ball in, ran, pumped again, twisted, had Vickers and Curry knock each other off the play as they collided, then spotted Salido sneaking across the end zone."

Ty Detmer not only carved up the Hurricanes, but often he did it on the dead run after scrambling away from a furious Miami rush.

As heroic as Ty Detmer might have been in the win over Miami, it was the Cougar defense that held the fort down the stretch.

Bedlam in Provo: The Cougars' victory over cocky, trash-talking Miami set off a wave of excitement among BYU fans and it marked the school's first-ever win against a No. 1-ranked team.

This was vintage Detmer, and if any one magic act won Ty the Heisman Trophy in 1990, that was it.

Back on the field, Detmer played Houdini again on the two-point conversion try, bootlegging around end and firing a pass to Boyce.

BYU led 28–21 and had dominated the overconfident Canes.

Miami didn't really die easily that night. Twice in the fourth quarter, Erickson shrugged off his complaining teammates and threw potential touchdown passes.

One more BYU hero stepped forward and played his way to glory on national television. Cougar cornerback Ervin Lee, the lightest player on the BYU squad, intercepted Erickson in the end zone to kill one drive and then, in the closing minutes of the game, Lee tipped away a fourth-down pass inside BYU's 5-yard line.

When the clock wound down, BYU fans bolted down from the stands, hopping over guard rails, rushing down ramps, flooding the field. It was the most emotional scene at a sports event in state history. Police guarded the goal posts as students hopped onto each other's shoulders. Others mobbed the team.

By the numbers: Detmer completed 38 of 54 passes for 406 yards and three touchdowns, earning all the respect the Canes had wished to deny him.

Edwards, who has been at the top, who has a national championship trophy in his office, thought he'd seen it all.

"If someone would have told me we would have six turnovers and beat Miami, I'd have asked to give him a saliva test," he said.

Finally, the national media seemed to cotton to the idea that BYU was for real.

And certainly that Detmer was something special.

"If he isn't Heisman Trophy stuff, there's not a Mormon in Utah," wrote Edwin Pope for the *Miami Herald.*

Russ White of the *Orlando Sentinel* had the funniest, and maybe most accurate summation, of Detmer's unbelievable evening: "That is the single best performance I have ever seen. This has to be the earliest they've awarded the Heisman Trophy. I gave it to him in my third paragraph."

At last, for recognition-starved BYU, the world had come to the Wasatch and learned once and for all that the Cougars could play.

Case closed.

10
N
64
LOMAX
31
J. JOHNSON
59
CONDIE
95
POCHMAN

CHAPTER

SEVEN

Having to deal with the issue of missionaries leaving and coming back to school without a football mentality, or not at all, was supposed to be one the reasons BYU couldn't be a big-time football power. But coach Edwards' positive spin on the situation changed that outlook forever.

Men on a

"... I THINK THE TWO GREATEST SACRIFICES A MAN COULD MAKE IS TO GO ON A MISSION OR BE A CATHOLIC PRIEST."

—STEVE SARKISIAN
'97 BYU QUARTERBACK

Mission

CHRIS PELLA spent 18 years at Utah State, two of them as head coach. Pella generally experienced nothing but frustration coaching against instate rival BYU.

Why?

"I've thought a lot about it over the years," said Pella, who is now BYU's recruiting coordinator. "I've always wondered why BYU has won so many championships, dominated rivals and gone to bowl games over the years. I think I know. It's because of character.

"By and large, BYU's football players have a lot of character. They know how to win. It's a feeling. They're young men who have a sense of where they came from, where they are and what they want to accomplish. I call it character."

For years, the Cougars have been teased for their goodie-goodie image. And when a BYU player stumbles, the fallout from media attention is nearly quadruple what it would be at other schools.

The Cougs played in, and won, the first WAC championship game in 1996.

"And that's to be expected," BYU athletic director Rondo Fehlberg said. "If we set a standard for ourselves, people want to hold us to the bar. When we fail, it disappoints us more than anyone else. But we keep the bar raised and shoot for it."

One of the biggest character-builders for so many Cougar athletes has been their calling to LDS Church missions.

But it wasn't always that way.

The relationship between BYU and the LDS Church will always remain in place. It affects LaVell Edwards and the program in many ways, including recruiting in the Hawaiian islands, where there is a significant LDS presence.

Before LaVell Edwards took the BYU head coaching job in 1972, the Cougar football program had experienced little success, and missions were viewed as one of the stumbling blocks.

Edwards turned that around. Now most of BYU's Mormon athletes—normally about two-thirds of the football team—serve two- year missions, as recommended by the Church of Jesus Christ of Latter-day Saints.

The service is voluntary, not required. When young men reach the age of 19, they can apply to serve a mission. If accepted, they receive a call which could send them anywhere from California to a third world country. And in the '90s, even to Russia.

Athletes who serve missions do mature physically, emotionally and spiritually. But those attributes are not always a benefit, as many of BYU's critics argue.

Some missionaries return and have no desire to play football again. Others have come back with life-threatening diseases which have caused lifelong problems.

Taking this issue of missionary service, turning it into a positive, and balancing the line between aggressive football and those feelings of humility, peace and love which missionary service requires of a young man isn't always so easy.

Marty Roosendahl left BYU for an LDS Mission in the early '90s following an All-America football career at Ricks JC. At the time of his departure, he was 6-foot-5 and weighed 300 pounds. He could play any position on the offensive line.

When Roosendahl returned home two years later, he weighed 190 pounds. His desire to continue football waned. His priorities had changed.

Roosendahl never played a down of football for the Cougars. Yet on Edwards staff, such athletes are plugged into a complicated chart which tracks the coming and going of athletes with current recruiting efforts.

Skeptics in the NCAA—and certainly in the WAC—suggest that missionary service is a huge advantage for the Cougars. They want it curbed or banned, and the exemption from the NCAA five-year clock eliminated.

The naysayers' favorite expression, used with something less than admiration, is "religious redshirt"—as though BYU sends its promising young players off to spend two years at Gold's Gym.

If a guy serves a mission, critics insist, he should give up one or two years of his college eligibility.

BYU officials counter with the argument that if it is such an advantage to have players mature during LDS service, why don't more schools recruit Mormon athletes?

And when they do, why do they insist on mission service before enrolling in school?

Missionaries have surfaced at Utah's instate colleges more and more in recent years as the LDS Church has grown. Many other schools, including Colorado State, Arizona State, Wisconsin, Wyoming and others have seen returned missionaries star for their football teams.

But generally, these schools avoid recruiting Mormons who say they will go on two-year missions, especially if they might consider interrupting their football careers.

Yet no one would argue the point that missions do build character. And the athletes who benefit most physically from the extra two years are offensive and defensive linemen.

Mormon missionaries do not spend the two years "working out" or housed in a training camp that enhances their skills. Most preach the gospel in poverty-stricken countries, risking their lives in cultures where there is civil war, lack of structured authority or community peace.

Missionaries have been killed in South America, Ireland and other places by gunfire and random attacks.

Mormon missionaries have been threatened, beaten, and witnessed abuses, hunger, starvation and natural calamities like earthquakes, hurricanes and volcanic eruptions—such as the one that struck the Phillipines near Manila.

Steve Sarkisian, the quarterback who led BYU to the 1997 Cotton Bowl victory over Kansas State, is not a Mormon.

"But I think the two greatest sacrifices a man could make is to go on a mission or be a Catholic priest," Sarkisian said.

Although missionaries do a lot of walking and can often be seen riding bikes in most cities in the world, that

LDS Church missionary Dustin Johnson returned to BYU in time to play fullback on the 1996 team that went 14-1 and was ranked fifth in the nation. The coaching staff moved Johnson and his all-around athletic skills to tight end for the '97 season.

Paul Shoemaker, who was BYU's starting quarterback to open the 1997 season, had been away from competitive football for 3 years—redshirting one season and serving a two-year church mission.

exercise isn't enough to keep an athlete in playing shape for Division I football.

Most athletes "lose a feel" for football, and see their skills erode over two years. Their legs grow weak due to lack of sprinting, jumping and stretching the fast-twitching muscle fibers.

Studies have proven that when BYU missionary-athletes return to Provo, it takes an average of eight months to regain a sense of athletic confidence.

That's a long time in the cauldron of Division I competition.

"On a mission, the whole point is to love everybody," said receiver Cliff Doman, one of four Doman brothers to play at BYU and serve as missionaries. "You're serving people. You've been loving people for two years and then you've got to come back and destroy the guy across from you.

"That's what you have to do if you're going to be good in football. You've got to have that fighter instinct in you, and that was hard to get back."

Chuck Cutler, a receiver who caught darts from Ty Detmer, once delivered a baby on a dirt floor in Ecuador. He used a kitchen knife to cut the umbilical cord and the appreciative parents nicknamed the baby girl "Chuckcita."

Cutler, who led the team in receiving in 1988, once ate dog meat, trying not to offend the local people. Because Cutler served his mission from 1983–85, he sacrificed being a member of the 1984 national championship team. He also contracted a tapeworm that threatened his life and kept him from keeping weight on all during his football career.

For LaVell Edwards, the mission thing is always a balancing act. Like a gift box, it usually presents surprises. Edwards has seen athletes serve missions, return and excel both on the field and in life.

He's also seen athletes return from missions, fail on the field and in life, even die early from drug addiction or in accidents.

Edwards has seen athletes return

from missionary service with anything remotely resembling feistiness drained completely from their systems.

"We know we're far from perfect," offensive lineman and returned missionary Eric Bateman said following BYU's 14-1 season in 1996. "One thing I can honestly say is that we're striving to be. We want to be good. We want to succeed."

Because of missionary service, LaVell Edwards rarely has more than 75 scholarship players on the field during a season. Sell that to Miami, Ohio State or Texas.

"We don't always know who is going, or when," running back coach Lance Reynolds said. "A player will come in as a freshman and say he's not going to go on a mission. Then he turns 19 and comes in and tells us he is going two months from now. The planning is the hard part."

When offensive line coach Roger French first saw a local Mormon kid named Eli Herring, he got excited.

Herring, a high school shot put champion, was 6-8 and 320 pounds. Herring went on a mission, returned, and was a star for BYU in the early '90s.

But Herring never took football that seriously.

When his senior year ended in 1994, Herring drew national attention by writing letters to NFL teams, asking them not to waste their draft picks on him.

Herring later explained that he had no desire to play football on Sunday. He considered playing on Sunday a distraction from a day of worship.

Despite his letters, the Raiders drafted Herring anyway—hoping they could convert him by giving him a sales job or dangling money in front of his face.

Defensive lineman Bryon Frisch returned from his mission to become a force on the BYU Cotton Bowl champs of 1996.

Herring would not bite.

The Herring story, chronicled by the *Associated Press, USA Today* and features in newspapers like the *Los Angeles Times,* stands as a reminder that when pushed to the spiritual letter, some BYU football players push back.

Football, at least for Herring, was never the means to an end. It was an experience that ended the day Saturday play was over. In a nutshell, Herring had character. And he would not compromise his principles.

"If they ever change to Saturdays, I'd be very interested," Herring told the media.

The Raiders, while saying they respected Herring's beliefs, went after Herring anyway in the spring of 1995. Team executive Bruce Allen flew to Utah and talked to Herring about the kinds of contracts second-round draft choices received that year.

The Raiders would have paid Herring $500,000 per season for as many as three years. Herring had a wife and was starting a family. Money was tight. His salary as a teacher would be about $22,000 a year.

"On a mission, the whole point is to love everybody, you're serving people. You've been loving people for two years and then you've got to come back and destroy the guy across from you . . . that's what you have to do if you're going to be good in football."

– Cliff Doman
BYU receiver and
one of four Doman brothers
to play at BYU and serve
as missionaries

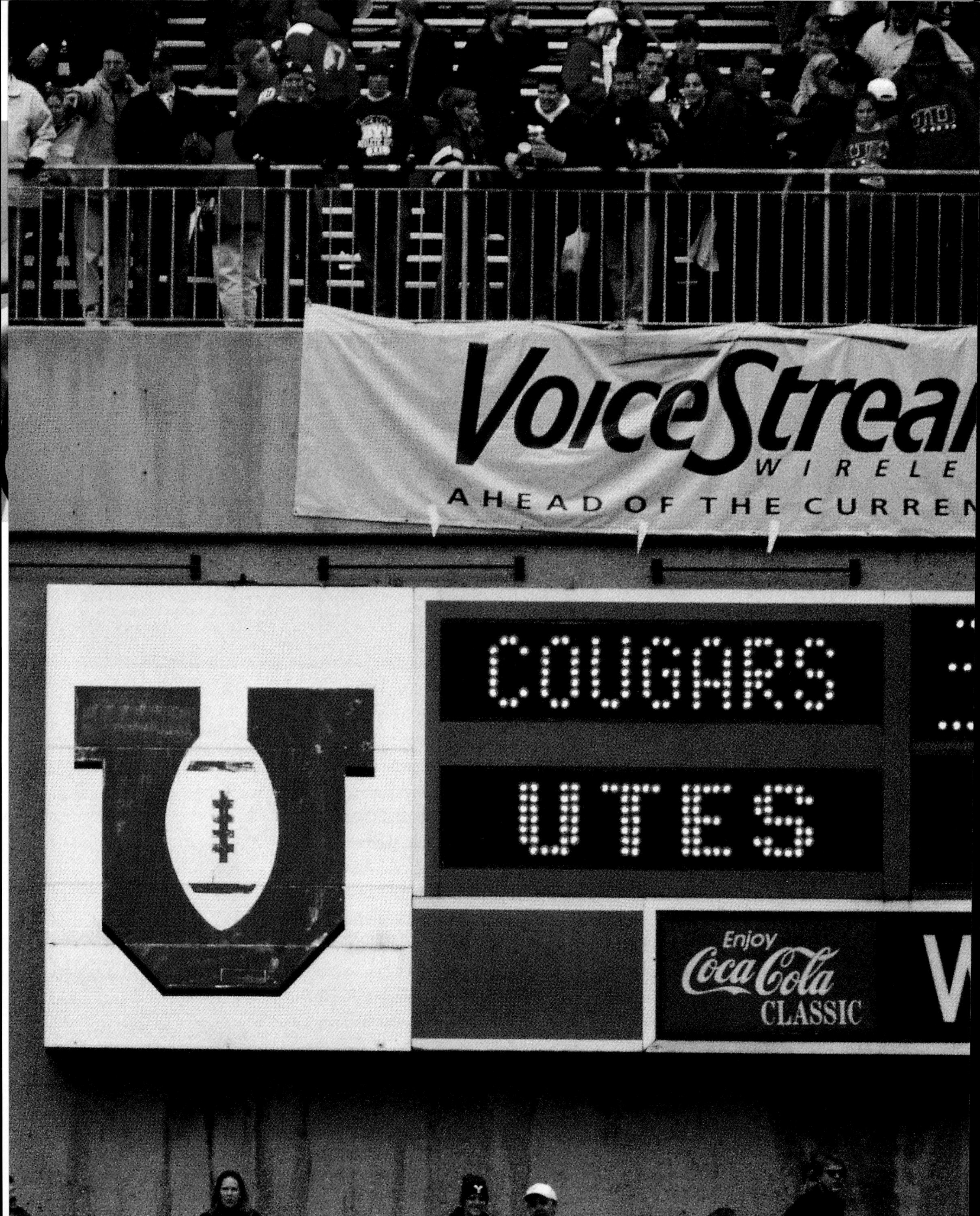
VoiceStrea
WIRELE
AHEAD OF THE CURREN
COUGARS
UTES
Enjoy
Coca-Cola
CLASSIC

Stats & Records

Football Lettermen

Abbott, Fielding	1946–47
Adams, Doug	1972–74
Adams, John	1981
Adams, Richard	1967–69
Adams, Tim	1989
Affleck, Dave	1972–73
Ah You, Charlie	1973–75
Ah You, Harland	1995–present
Aitken, Ray	1949
Akeo, Ladd	1984–86
Akerfelds, Daniel	1982–83
Albrecht, Scott	1994
Alexander, Payton	1926–27
Alger, Ned	1950
Allen, Bill	1974–75
Allen, Eddie	1936–37
Allen, Mark	1983–84
Allen, Marvin	1978, '81–84
Allen, Paul	1960–61
Allphin, Bob	1964–65
Allphin, Dave	1965–67
Allred, Art	1969–70
Allred, Mart	1956
Ambrosius, Joe	1995–present
Anae, Brad	1980–81
Anae, Famika	1954–55
Anae, Robert	1982–84
Andersen, Jason	1994–present
Andersen, Rj	1996–present
Anderson, John	1949
Anderson, Kenneth	1924
Anderson, LeGrande	1925–26
Anderson, Mel	1941
Anderson, Neil	1982–83
Anderson, Rob	1979–80
Anderson, Steve	1982
Anderson, Tyler	1988, '92–93
Andrews, Regan	1981–83
Andrus, Lou	1965–66
Ane, Neal	1976
Apostol, Kip	1976–77
Armstrong, Bob	1982–83
Arnold, Josh	1988–91
Asay, Bert	1934–35
Ash, Wayne	1956
Ashdown, Bob	1964–66
Ashman, John	1990
Atkinson, Dave	1971–73
Atuaia, Donny	1996–present
Atuaia, Mark	1991, '94–96
August, Bill	1971–72
Aupiu, David	1979–82
Autentico, Randy	1963
Awai, Barrett	1991–92
Badger, Lonnie	1953
Bailey, Joe	1971–73
Bailey, Mike	1971
Baker, Frank	1961–63
Baker, Wayne	1972–74
Baldwin, Tom	1993–95
Balholm, Neil	1981–82
Ball, Jason	1993
Ballard, Jim	1963
Ballif, Ariel	1924
Ballif, Jae	1950–52
Ballif, Mark	1929
Balmforth, Jim	1988–90
Baltzer, Tom	1966–67
Banker, Carl	1962–63
Banky, Richard	1965–67
Banzhaf, Steve	1970
Barrow, Bob	1961–63
Barrus, Dave	1959
Basinger, Earl	1927
Bateman, Eric	1995–present
Bateman, Fred	1939–40
Bateman, Max	1936–37
Bates, Derick	1995–present
Bates, Layne	1989
Bean, Bob	1966–67
Bean, Larry	1952
Bean, Ron	1943–54
Beatty, Bryon	1989
Bechtold, John	1983
Beckstead, Chad	1936–38
Beckstrom, Mark	1949
Bell, Tom	1977–79
Bellini, Mark	1982, 84–86
Bellini, Matt	1987–90
Belnap, Bud	1960
Bench, Dean	1925
Benson, Don	1948–50
Bergeson, Eric	1988–89
Berry, Rex	1948–50
Berntsen, Mark	1975–77
Bertotti, George	1932
Betham, John	1972–74
Biddulph, Floyd	1931–32
Biddulph, Buddy	1925
Biddy, Bob	1975–76
Biegel, Rocky	1988–91
Biegel, T.D.	1993–94
Billick, Brian	1974–76
Bills, Bob	1951
Bills, Karol	1949, '52
Bingham, Neil	1968–70
Bird, Forest	1936–38
Bird, Ken	1941–42
Bird, Nick	1923
Bisgaard, Christopher	1995–96
Bisho, Chris	1986, '87
Blackham, Gordon	1964–65
Blackham, Shirl	1939–40
Blackwell, Clay	1978–79
Blanc, Jeff	1973–76
Bloomfield, Henry	1995–96
Bloomfield, Tefua	1994–95
Boardman, Alan	1993–96
Bolli, Tyler	1993–96
Borgia, John	1984–87
Bosco, Angelo	1951
Bosco, Robbie	1983–85
Boulter, Roy	1947
Bower, Wayne	1971–73
Bowers, Carl	1969–71
Bowers, Dan	1969–71
Bowers, Wesley	1942
Bowman, Bernardino	1922–24
Bowman, George	1951–53
Bowman, Spero	1970–71
Boyce, Andy	1988–90
Boyette, Casey	1966–68
Bozich, Craig	1966–68
Bradford, Perry	1978
Brady, Mark	1979–81
Brady, Mike	1960–62
Brady, Phil	1962–64
Brady, Steve	1980–81
Braga, Matt	1979–80
Bray, Ken	1963–65
Brewster, Dennis	1963–65
Brink, Lloyd	1938–40
Brinley, Eldon	1928–30
Brock, Randy	1991–94
Brooks, Dave	1971–73
Brooks, Michael	1988
Brown, Clay	1978–80
Brown, Curtis	1958
Brown, R.K.	1957–58
Brown, Reed	1976
Brumfield, Scott	1991–92
Brundage, Dewey	1951–53
Bryant, Bill	1990–92
Buchanan, Rob	1978–79
Buck, Jason	1985–86
Bulloch, Burt	1956
Bunker, Carl	1962–63
Bunnell, Karl	1927–29
Bunnell, Merrill	1922–23
Burningham, Rex	1982–83
Burr, Bruce	1950
Busenbark, Don	1986–88
Bushore, Don	1946–49
Buswell, Blair	1981
Butler, Tony	1982
Buys, Joseph	1926–28
Bybee, Royce	1979–80
Cabulagan, Pat	1981–83
Cahoon, Ben	1996–present
Cahoon, Brad	1986–87
Caldwell, Paul	1955–58
Call, Dee	1942
Call, Ken	1967–68
Campora, Steve	1956
Campos, Dave	1977
Cannon, Curt	1996–present

Carlile, Alan	1977
Carlson, Chuck	1974–76
Carlson, Clark	1973–75
Carlson, Kent	1986
Carlson, Steve	1979–80
Carr, Larry	1972–74
Carter, Virgil	1964–66
Carter, Ross	1952
Chadwick, Dave	1948–49, '52
Chaffetz, Jason	1988–89
Chamberlain, Garth	1939–41
Chamberlain, Royal	1922
Chamberlain, Royal	1992–93
Charlton, Scott	1989–91
Chatterton, Marc	1942
Chatterton, Marcell	1946
Chipman, Dee	1939–41
Chitty, Leonard	1986–87
Chow, Warren	1987
Christensen, Jack	1936–38
Christensen, John	1990–91
Christensen, Rex	1937
Christensen, Steve	1968
Christensen, Steve	1992–93
Christensen, Todd	1974–77
Christianson, Frank	1992–93
Christopoulos, Tony	1949
Chronister, Mike	1976–78
Clark, Brad	1989–92
Clark, Glen	1946–49
Clark, Tim	1986–88
Clark, Tom	1956–57
Clarke, Willard	1925–26
Clements, Steve	1992–94
Close, Calvin	1977, '80–81
Clove, Alvie	1949–50
Cobabe, John	1954
Coggins, Deven	1988–89
Cole, Tom	1959
Collie, Scott	1979–82
Coloma, Jason	1976–78
Colson, Terry	1965–67
Colvin, Reed	1927
Condie, Brandon	1996–present
Condie, Howard	1957
Condie, Vernon	1931–33
Conners, Chris	1990–91
Conrad, Mike	1961–63
Cook, Ben	1995–present
Cook, Cory	1993–94
Cook, Jamie	1994–95
Cook, Jerry	1965–67
Cook, Wayne	1934–35
Coon, Dave	1970–71, '73
Coon, Doug	1972
Cooper, George	1930
Cooper, Jason	1993–95
Corbett, Don	1924–27
Corbett, George	1927
Corchnoy, Barry	1962–64
Corless, Albert	1927
Corley, Stacey	1988–90
Corson, Steve	1977
Covey, Sean	1987–89
Cox, Matt	1995–present
Crandall, Ray	1971
Crane, Reed	1935–36
Criddle, Jesse	1950
Crittenden, Jim	1954–55
Crompton, Craig	1970–72
Crowe, Chris	1974–75
Crutchfield, Tony	1988–91
Cunningham, Harold	1951–52
Cupp, Aaron	1995–present
Cutler, Chuck	1986–88
Dalebout, Paul	1956
Dalley, Alvin	1947–49
Daly, Ron	1949–50
Damuni, Jack	1993–94
Dangerfield, Steve	1960
Darling, Dick	1960–62
Dastrup, Andy	1928–30
Davis, Bill	1978–80
Davis, Bob	1987–89
Davis, Kirk	1987–88
Davis, Russ	1978
Dawson, Ted	1987–88, '92–93
Deavitt, Willard	1939
Decker, Merle	1946
Deeds, Keith	1947–49
Deeds, Scotty	1946–47
Dennis, Lonnie	1957–59
Denny, Craig	1971–73
DeSantis, Steve	1990
Detmer, Ty	1988–91
Dewey, Steve	1974–76
Dignan, Tom	1974–75
Dimick, Bob	1949–50
Dixon, Sanky	1926–28
Dixon, Donald Jr.	1955–57
Dixon, Buck	1922–25
Dixon, Norm	1988–90
Dixon, Owen	1939–41, '46
Dixon, Rick	1967–69
Doerr, Dick	1949
Doman, Bryce	1988, 92–94
Doman, Cliff	1996–present
Doman, Dennis	1970–71
Doman, Kevin	1985–86
Doney, Darrell	1950–52
Dow, Mac	1936
Dowell, John	1976
Drage, Eric	1990–93
Duerden, Verle	1949
Dugger, Jerry	1971
Duke, Dev	1973–74, '77
Dunn, Gary	1959
Dupaix, Roger	1960–62
Duran, Dave	1965
Durrant, Jim	1934
Duva, Jeff	1975
Dvorak, Bill	1970–71
Dyches, Ronald	1928–30
Dye, James	1995–96
Dyer, Lee	1942
Earp, Robert	1952
Eccles, Jim	1947–49
EchoHawk, Larry	1968–69
EchoHawk, Tom	1972–73
Eckel, Paul	1957–58
Eddo, Mike	1982–83
Edwards, Jimmy	1981, '84–86
Edwards, Jim	1989, '92–94
Egbert, Hal	1948
Egbert, Wendell	1952
Eggertsen, Armand	1931–32
Ehin, Chuck	1979–82
Ehrmann, Paul	1965–66
Eldredge, Lloyd	1980–82
Elewonibi, Mo	1988–89
Ellis, Jeff	1995–present
Empey, Mike	1987, '91–93
Enlow, Tom	1977–78
Erdhaus, John	1967
Evans, Joe	1990–91
Eyre, DeRay	1951–53
Eyre, Nick	1976, 78–80
Faalufua, Wayne	1981–82
Facer, Steve	1969–71
Fairbanks, Lloyd	1973–74
Fannin, Scott	1996
Farasopoulos, Chris	1968–70
Farmer, Lance	1991
Farmer, Scott	1956
Farner, Nairne	1962–63
Farnsworth, Harold	1972–73
Faulkner, Jim	1969–70
Faupula, Elias	1994–95
Favero, Dewey	1933–34
Felt, Dick	1952–54
Fenessy, Bob	1953
Fennegan, Garth	1992
Feterik, Kevin	1996–present
Fifita, Kalani	1994
Filiaga, Pulusila	1979–81
Finai, Pisa	1975
Finfrock, Dennis	1969
Fitisemanu, Alema	'85,'87,'89–90
Flaherty, Bob	1951
Flammer, Mark	1978
Fleming, Lucky Dare	1969–70
Flint, Brandon	1981–83
Foreman, Nate	1996–present
Fort, Neal	1987, 89–90
Fortie, Eldon	1960–62
Fowler, Blaine	1983–85
Francis, Dave	1978–80
Frandsen, Jeff	1987–89
Frankovich, George	1952
Frantz, Gene	1960–62
Frazier, Danny	1977
Frazier, Dion	1960–63
Frazier, Sid	1965–67
Freeland, Jim	1994–95
Frisch, Byron	1996–present
Fuller, Boney	1922–26
Fuller, Troy	1986–89
Furstenau, Todd	1995
Futrell, David	1984–87
Garber, Jon	1989–90
Gardner, Dean	1939–40
Gardner, Glenn	1965–66
Gardner, Morris	1946
Garrick, Craig	1982–84
Gaspard, Al	1977–78
Germann, Chris	1986–87
Gibbs, Nathan	1992–94
Gifford, Jack	1960
Gilbert, Art	1938, '40
Giles, Earl	1935
Giles, Mark	1973–75
Giles, Scott	1990–91
Gillenwater, Gil	1972–73
Gillespie, George	1932–34
Gillespie, Gerald	1935–37
Gillespie, Horace	1946–49
Giordano, Gabe	1995–present
Giordano, Philip	1994–present
Gledhill, Elwood	1923–24
Glatch, Bill	1969–70
Gomes, Lenny	1991–93
Gomm, Ken	1954
Gourley, George	1971–72
Gourley, Roger	1975–77
Gouveia, Kurt	1983–85
Gravelle, Gordon	1968–69
Gray, Derwin	1989–92
Green, Eddie	1987, 89
Greene, John	1965
Griffin, Don	1968–70
Griffith, Kent	1989–91
Griffith, Melvin	1930–32
Griffitts, Bobby	1993
Gruber, George	1967–69
Gulstad, Chris	1992
Gunderson, Brian	1970–71
Gunther, Kurt	1980–82
Gustavson, Paul	1973

Football Lettermen

Hadfield, Mark	1994
Hahn, Gary	1975–76
Hale, Guy	1962–64
Hale, Lane	1994–96
Hales, Iman	1931
Hall, Jan	1968
Hall, Kalin	1992–93
Hall, Marshall	1961–62
Hall, Nathan	1992–93
Hall, Steve	1969–70
Hall, Travis	1991–94
Halvorson, Tim	1975, '78–79
Hamblin, Bob	1951–52
Hamblin, Jay	1948–50
Hamilton, Larry	1982–84
Hamilton, Waymon	1980–83
Hancock, Larry	1950–52
Hancock, Ryan	1991–92
Handley, Darren	1986–88
Hanks, Dave	1956
Hanks, Wayne	1933
Hanna, Sam	1968
Hansen, Bill	1994–95
Hansen, Brian	1978, '81–82
Hansen, Bruce	1981, '85–86
Hansen, Dan	1970–72
Hansen, Danny	1977–79
Hansen, Regan	1986–88
Hansen, Shad	1989–92
Hanshaw, Tim	1992–94
Hapi, Joe	1931
Hardisty, Brad	1982
Hardy, Ariel	1937
Hardy, Merrill	1948–49, '53
Harmann, Gary	1968–69
Harmer, Larry	1994
Harn, Gary	1967–69
Harper, Steve	1982–83
Harrington, Alema	1986–88
Harrington, Tau	1988, 90
Harris, Carl	1924, '26
Harris, George	1975–77
Harris, Jeff	1977–78
Harris, Kelly	1976–77
Harston, Pete	1988–90
Hart, Kay	1932–34
Hartwig, Dan	1977
Harvey, James	1990
Hatch, Victor	1922
Hawkins, Harold	1959
Hawkins, Wally	1967–68
Haycock, Bevan	1949
Haymond, Steve	1983–84
Haysbert, Adam	1983–84
Heaps, Larry	1968–70
Hecker, Jim	1942
Heggins, James	1994
Heimuli, Hema	1992–95
Heimuli, Lakei	1983–86
Heinz, Lyle	1954
Henderson, Dave	1989–91
Herget, Todd	1991–93
Hernandez, Tony	1976–77
Herrick, Joe	1991–93
Herring, Eli	1987, '91 94
Herrmann, Jim	1981, '83–84
Hess, Dean	1939–40
Hickman, Wayland	1993–94
Hill, Dick	1948–50
Hinckley, Fritz	1923–25
Hinckley, Mike	1955
Hoagland, Greg	1996–present
Hobbs, Richard	1985–87
Hoge, Chris	1988
Hoggan, Mike	1985, '90–91
Holle, Kirk	1990
Holman, Howard	1959
Holmoe, Tom	1979–82
Holt, Gayle	1946–48
Homolik, Wes	1967, '69–70
Hoover, Bliss	1928–30
Hopkins, Tom	1981–82
Horlacher, Fred	1931
Howard, Bob	1923–25
Howard, Paul	1970–71
Hubbard, Dave	1974–76
Hubbs, Keith	1957
Huber, Max	1965–67
Huckaby, Jay	1985–87
Hudson, Gordon	1981–83
Hughes, Brian	1993–94
Hughes, Erik	1991–92
Hullinger, Jess	1923–24
Hulse, Clarence	1952
Hunt, Ed	1956
Hunt, Kahlili	1972–73
Hunter, Brad	1986, '90–92
Hunter, Greg	1987–88
Hunter, John	1985–88
Hunter, Logan	1971–72
Hutchins, Aaron	1996
Hutchinson, Grant	1932–34
Hyder, John	1969–70
Ieremia, Mekeli	1974–77
Imboden, Earl	1946
Jackson, Elwood	1922
Jackson, George	1940
Jackson, Kip	1968–70
Jackson, Weldon	1956–58
Jacobsen, Lloyd	1966–67
Jacobsen, Mike	1962–64
Jacobsen, Mike	1968–70
Jacobson, Ron	1956
James, Don	1953–54
James, Joe	1967
Jaramillo, Jim	1978–80
Jenkins, Ronney	1996–present
Jenkins, Mike	1990–91
Jenne, Bruce	1990–92
Jennings, Gordon	1964–66
Jensen, Blake	1982–83
Jensen, Bob	1986–87
Jensen, Craig	1974–76
Jensen, Ken	1939
Jensen, Michael	1980–82
Jensen, Phil	1972–75
Jensen, Roland	1939–40
Jeppesen, Garen	1987–88
Jewkes, Jackson	1936–38
John, Delmar	1941
Johnson, Brent	1978–79
Johnson, Duane	1987–89
Johnson, Dustin	1995
Johnson, James	1993–96
Johnson, Lee	1981–84
Johnson, Louis	1930–31
Johnson, Malcolm	1934
Johnson, Merrill	1960
Johnson, Sid	1979
Johnston, Carroll	1956–57
Johnston, Mike	1992–95
Jones, Charles	1996–present
Jones, Homer	1979–80
Jones, Jimmy	1981–82
Jones, Lloyd	1978–80
Jones, Monte	1963–65
Jones, Rick	1968, '70
Jones, Richard	1977
Jones, Robert	1963
Jones, Roy	1956
Jorgensen, Todd	1992

Kama, Gary	1975–77, '79
Kanahele, Marcus	1975–76
Kapele, John	1957–59
Kapele, John	1987
Karpowitz, Bob	1949–51
Katoa, Andy	1985–86
Katoa, Fotu	1989
Katoa, Fred	1990
Kauffman, Earl	1988–91
Kaufusi, Rich	1989–90
Kaufusi, Steve	1986–87
Kawaa, John	1962–63
Kealaluhi, K.O.	1995–96
Kehl, Ed	1995–present
Keim, Mike	1988–90
Keitzman, Jim	1946–47
Kellermeyer, Doug	1981–83
Kennedy, Jared	1996–present
Kim, Moses	1964–66
Kimball, Edwin	1923–24
Kimball, Tim	1948–49
Kimball, Tom	1938
Kimball, Warren	1951
Kimmel, Jim	1962–64
Kinard, David	1985, '89–91
Kinder, George	1958
King, David	1984–86
Kiscr, Larry	1987
Kline, Dan	1966
Knight, Ron	1970–71
Knight, Shawn	1983–86
Knight, Tim	1986–88
Knight, William	1994
Knoblauch, Paul	1962–64
Knowles, Chad	1992–94
Knudsen, Clarence	1924–26
Knudsen, Moyle	1936, '38
Kochevar, Lewis	1950–51
Kochevar, Paul	1953–54
Koller, Lyle	1946–1949
Kormylo, John	1978
Kozlowski, Glen	1981, '83–85
Kuhlman, Bill	1956
Lacey, Mike	1979–81
LaComb, Frank	1932–34
LaComb, Gary	1954–55
Ladd, Tom	1989–91
Lahmann, Tom	1966–68
Lamb, Ed	1995–96
Lambert, Darrin	1987
Lane, Eric	1979–80
Larsen, Bob	1971–73
Latimer, Don	1954
Lauder, David	1992, '94
Laverty, Ben	1965–66
Leavitt, Fred	1955, '59
Leavitt, Hafen	1939
Leavitt, Jared	1990–91
Ledbetter, Lennon	1991
Ledenko, Rob	1983–84
Lee, Ervin	1989–91
Leeper, Bill	1967–68
Lefevre, Reg	1939–40
Legas, Dick	1968
Leonard, Drew	1937–38
Lever, Keith	1990–91
Lewis, Burnell	1931
Lewis, Chad	1993–96
Lewis, Gail	1939–41
Liapis, Pete	1946
Liday, Bob	1942
Liljenquist, Joe	1969–71
Linder, Jack	1961
Lindley, Lance	1984–85
Lindquist, Ed	1963
Lindsley, Steve	1985–86

Lindstrom, Dave	1949, '52
Lindstrom, Jeff	1993
Linford, Frank	1974
Linford, Jay	1983
Linford, Paul	1972–74
Linford, Ray	1978–80
Litchfield, Randy	1973
Livingston, Jeff	1961–63
Livingston, Joe	1973
Lloyd, Cecil	1948–1949
Lloyd, Don	1925
Lloyd, Vaughn	1935–1938
Lloyd, Wesley	1925
Lobue, Sam	1973–74
Lomax, Desmond	1996–present
Long, Rod	1948–1950
Long, Troy	1985–88
Longhurst, Herman	1940–42
Loper, Mike	1966–68
Lopez, Richard	1966–68
Loose, Bob	1954
Lott, Dean	1986–87
Loveless, Elmer	1928–1929
Lowry, Dave	1974–76
Lupoi, John	1967–69
Lundberg, Jerry	1952
Lyman, Jeff	1969–70
Lyons, Marc	1967–69
Lyons, Walter	1935
Madsen, Lovell	1950–52
Maeser, Meith	1922
Magalei, Issiah	1996–present
Magalei, Shane	1996–present
Magleby, Francis	1948–49
Magleby, Russell	1928–1930
Magoffin, Dick	1959
Mahoney, Tim	1974
Malarsie, John	1961–63
Mannion, John	1981–82
Manson, Hunter	1922–23
Manson, Judd	1930–32
Manwill, Walt	1978–81
Marchello, Ivan	1989
Marking, Jerry	1940–41
Marriott, Bill	1962–64
Marriott, Todd	1988
Marshall, Bob	1963–64
Martin, Brad	1995–present
Martin, Drayton	1990
Martini, Ralph	1987
Martinez, Joe	1952, '55
Matau, Chris	1985–86
Mathie, Lynn	1962–63
Matich, Trevor	1979–80, '83–84
Matsuzaki, Micah	1989–91, '93
Matthews, Bill	1956
Matthews, Blaine	1983
Matthews, Keith	1950–52
Matthews, Weldon	1930–33
Mattingly, Ty	1985–86
Mavrakis, Sam	1939, '41
May, Bryan	1989–91
Maynard, Ken	1940
Mazorra, Dennis	1981–82
Mazzotta, Casey	1992–93
McBeth, Paul	1935–1937
McBeth, Travis	1987–88
McCluskey, Mark	1974–75
McCorquindale, John	1976
McCullough, Hassan	1992
McCullough, Keith	1984–85
McDade, Jim	1983–84
McDonald, Jay	1984–85
McEwen, Terry	1976–77
McFarlane, Nyle	1958
McGinn, Joe	1958–59
McGuire, Kaipo	1993–96
McIntosh, Kimball	1924
McKee, Dave	1977–78, '81
McKenzie, Brian	1996–present
McLaren, Dave	1955
McMahon, Jim	1977–78, '80–81
McNabb, Bill	1982–83
McNaughton, Austin	1964
McTyer, Tim	1995–96
McWhorter, George	1949–50
Meadows, Billy	1953
Mees, Mike	1979, '81–82
Mendenhall, Pete	1923–26
Mendenhall, Mat	1975–79
Mendenhall, Paul	1953–54
Mendenhall, Ron	1969–70
Mendenhall, Wilford	1923–24
Mercado, Hank	1968
Merkeley, Floyd	1933–34
Merkley, Cecil	1924–25
Merkley, Doran	1961–63
Merkley, Scott	1992–94
Merrill, Kimball	1946–48
Merrill, Ray	1929–31
Meservey, Matt	1989, '92–95
Meteer, Dave	1974–76
Meyer, Gerald	1968–70
Miles, David	1985–87
Mili, Itula	1991, '94–96
Miller, Bill	1969–71
Miller, Jay	1972–74, '76
Miller, Larry	1975–78
Miller, Lynn	1922
Miller, Steve	1975–76
Miller, Tom	1977–78
Miller, Val	1972–73
Millet, Floyd	1932–33
Mills, Dave	1981, '83–84
Mills, Mike	1940–42, '47
Mitchell, Brian	1987–90
Mitchell, Kevin	1983
Mitchell, Patrick	1991–94
Mitton, Bill	1964–65
Moala, John	1996–present
Moberly, Scott	1990
Moeaki, John	1994
Moffat, Chad	1988, '91
Molifua, Wally	1972–73
Molini, Trevor	1984–86
Monahan, John	1970–72
Monson, Calvin	1953

Monson, Harold	1968
Moore, Larry	1995–96
Moore, Robert	1932
Morgan, Frank	1922
Morgan, Mike	1979–82
Morgan, Omarr	1996–present
Morrell, Kyle	1981–84
Morris, Rob	1993
Mortensen, Bennie	1950
Mortensen, Eric	1988–91
Muirbrook, Shay	1993–96
Mullenbrook, Grant	1941
Mulleneaux, Lynn	1962–63
Murdock, Blake	1973–76
Murdock, Bob	1988
Murdock, Steve	1931–32
Murdock, Steve	1947
Murphy, Lynn	1988
Murray, Mark	1936
Muse, Ivan	1953–54
Naiwahine, Henry	1964–65
Nance, Kent	1962, '64–65
Nash, Andrew	1993
Nauahi, Phil	1987–88
Neal, Ray	1954–56
Neal, John	1977, 79
Neal, Mark	1987–89
Neff, David	1981–84
Neilson, Scott	1977–79
Nelson, Bill	1961–63
Nelson, Ted	1969–70
Nelson, Tyler	1996–present
Newberry, Max	1965–67
Newell, Bob	1979
Nichols, Eddie	1969–70
Nicoll, Kevin	1991–92
Nielsen, Gifford	1975–77
Nielsen, Mel	1950–52
Nielsen, Wally	1950
Nilsen, Reed	1940–42, '46
Nilsson, Jeff	1974–76, '79
Nisonger, Hap	1931–33
Norberg, Scott	1984–85
Norton, Harold	1950
Nowatzke, Tim	1991–94
Nuckolls, Randy	1975
Nyberg, Brent	1989

Football Lettermen

Oaks, Charlie	1933–35
Oates, Barry	1980–82
Oates, Bart	1980–82
Oates, Brad	1973–75
Oates, John	1985
Oborn, Kent	1964–66
O'Brien, Mike	1986–88
Odle, Matt	1988–89
Odle, Phil	1965–67
Ofahangaue, Kelepi	'96–present
Ogden, John	1964–66
Ogden, Steve	1964–66
Oldroyd, Herman	1948
Oliverson, Glen	1942, '46–47
Oliverson, Ray	1950–51
Olsen, Orrin	1972, '74–75
Olsen, Rex	1946–47
Olson, Brent	1968
Olson, Mel	1964, '66, '69
Olson, Bob	1956–58
O'Neil, Mike	1980–82
Ongoongotau, Vaha	1994–95
Oramas, Sam	1983–84
Ord, Jon	1989–1992
Ormsby, Mark	1985
Orr, Bob	1941
Orr, Budd	1988–89
Orr, Richard	1984
Osborne, Bruce	1947–48
Overstreet, Leroy	1960
Oyler, Phil	1953–54

Packard, Paul	1922–1924
Pace, Corey	1980–81
Page, Max	1970–71
Palmer, Dennis	1964–66
Parker, Robert	1985–86
Parks, Noah	1995
Partridge, Truman	1922
Patera, Dennis	1967
Paterson, John	1967–69
Patterson, Craig	1987–89
Patton, Lyle	1948
Paulson, Art	1949, '51
Paulson, John	1949–50
Paxman, Gary	1950–52
Pay, Garry	1990–92
Paynter, Dean	1974
Pearson, Rich	1994
Pehrson, George	1935
Pendleton, Kirk	1981–83
Peterson, Ben	1995–96
Peterson, Gary	1975–77
Peterson, Greg	1981–83
Peterson, Lawrence	1925, '28
Peterson, Scott	1985–88
Peterson, Steve	1965–67
Pettis, Scott	1980–82
Phillips, Jim	1969–70
Phillips, Scott	1977–80
Pierce, Raynor	1956–57
Pilgrim, Evan	1991–94
Pistorius, Mike	1971–73
Pitts, Greg	1991–94
Pitts, Paul	1991
Plater, Dan	1978–81
Pochman, Ethan	1996
Pollard, Pearl	1929
Pollock, Jon	1993–94
Poodry, Bradley	1949–50
Popin, Bill	1976–77
Poppinga, Dennis	1970–71
Porter, Dave	1989–90
Porter, Ned	1949
Powers, Ralph	1954–55
Presley, Leo	1965–67
Prested, Bob	1977, '79–80
Preston, Mike	1971–73
Price, Roger	1986
Price, Steve	1971–73
Prince, Clement	1930
Probert, Leo	1929
Probert, Marion	1951–54

Raass, John	1994–95
Raass, Stan	1994–95
Ralph, Dick	1956
Ramage, John	1977, '80–81
Ransom, Villar	1942
Rasmussen, Korey	1984–86
Rawlinson, Doug	1985–86
Rawlinson, Randy	1983–84
Reading, Chris	1968–70
Reading, Lynn	1956
Reber, Scott	1977–79
Redd, Glenn	1979–80
Redden, Matt	1992–95
Reed, Dermmell	1994–95
Reed, Larry	1946
Reeve, Mark	1927–29
Reeve, Wayne	1939–40
Reid, Andy	1979–80
Reid, Spencer	1994–present
Regis, Larry	1956–57
Rex, Byron	1990–92
Reynolds, Lance	1972–73, '76–77
Rice, Bill	1974–76
Rice, Rodney	1987–88
Rice, Tom	1966
Richards, Golden	1970–71
Richards, Jimmy	1996–present
Richardson, Glen	1960–63
Richardson, Joe	1990
Richardson, Vernon	1930–32
Richins, Grant	1942
Ring, Bill	1977–78
Ringwood, Howard	1958–59
Ripee, Tom	1967–68
Riska, Gene	1939–41
Rivera, Keith	1971, '73–74
Roberts, Bobby	1965–67
Roberts, Charles	1936–38
Roberts, Kyle	1991–93
Roberts, Tim	1967–69
Robins, Roy	1973
Robinson, Alan	1962–64
Robinson, Chad	1987–89
Robinson, John	1953–54
Robinson, Scott	1983–85
Robison, Burle	1930–32
Rodoni, Brian	1985–87
Rodrique, Perry	1966–67
Rogers, Courtney	1986–88
Rogers, Steve	1980–81
Romero, Ed	1968
Romney, Golden	1925
Rossi, Pete	1984
Roundy, Elmo	1948–49, '52
Rowe, Owen	1926–28
Rozeshi, Ed	1971–72
Russell, Mike	1973–74
Russell, Tim	1965–66

Salanoa, Thor	1985–87
Salazar, Rob	1982–83
Salido, Mike	1987–88, '90
Saluone, Pili	1970–71
Saluone, Terence	1992–93
Samples, Bruce	1960
Samples, Gary	1965
Sampson, Eddie	1994–96
Sanders, Jack	1967
Sanders, Steve	1985–86
Sanford, Hunt	1932–34
Sanford, Terry	1967–68
Santiago, Lou	1963
Sarkisian, Steve	1995–96
Satterfield, LaVon	1951–53
Saunooke, Rob	1988
Scales, Roger	1967–68
Scanlan, Joe	1966–67
Schaerrer, Cade	1993
Schaffer, Max	1942
Schmidt, Jason	1991
Schmidt, Tom	1976
Schoepflin, Bill	1978–80
Schow, Doug	1964–66
Serck, Ken	1968–70
Shaw, Gary	1973–75
Shea, Glenn	1964–65
Sheide, Gary	1973–74
Shell, Todd	1980–83
Sherman, Marc	1984–85
Shields, Lloyd	1930–32
Shiffler, Mike	1996–present
Shifrer, Max	1946
Shober, Ernest	1930
Shoemaker, Paul	1995–present
Shumway, Drew	1953
Shumway, Jay	1984–86
Shumway, Shane	1984–86
Sikahema, Kapi	1991
Sikahema, Vai	1980–85
Simmerman, Bob	1977

Simmons, Dean	1933–34
Simmons, Dennis	1993–96
Simmons, Don	1926
Simmons, Gerald	1934
Simmons, Henry	1926–27
Simmons, Ron	1991–93
Simpson, Ron	1992
Sinclair, Paul	1987
Skidmore, Henry	1967–68
Skousen, Basil	1927–29
Skousen, Clarence	1927–28
Skousen, Jim	1946
Skousen, Marvin	1929–31
Skousen, Murray	1939
Skousen, Owen	1951–52
Slayton, Randy	1988–89
Slipp, Jeff	1967–69
Small, Mark	1990
Smilowitz, Julian	1972–73, '75
Smit, Walter	1950–52
Smith, Bennie	1971–72
Smith, Brad	1982–84
Smith, Bruce	1962–64
Smith, Chris	1987–90
Smith, Courtney	1996
Smith, Dave	1978–79
Smith, Horrace	1966–68
Smith, Kelly	1983–85
Smith, Ken	1984–85
Smith, Lloyd	1961–63
Smith, Mark	1988–90
Smith, Marlin	1958, '60
Smith, Sid	1972–75
Soffe, Ken	1936–38
Soffe, Wayne	1935–36
Spencer, Brock	1990
Sprouse, Al	1965
Sprowls, Jeff	1984–85
Squires, Monte	1966–68
Sralla, Scott	1991–93
St. Pierre, Ed	1978–80
Staley, Dustin	1995–96
Stapley, Hal	1956
Stapley, Stan	1946–47
Startin, Wayne	1956–58
Stearns, Ned	1996
Steele, Greg	1994
Stephens, Robert	1988–90
Sterling, Otis	1991–92
Stevens, Chris	1996–present
Stevenson, Derik	1995–96
Stewart, Ron	1963
Stinnett, Eddie	1982–83
Stoddard, Gary	1974
Stoddard, Troy	1993
Stolworthy, Reed	1949, 52–53
Stolworthy, Tom	1960
Stolworthy, Willard	1953–54
Stone, Devon	1961–63
Stone, Doug	1991–92
Stone, Thayne	1942, '46–48
Stratton, Steve	1971–73
Straw, Jason	1996–present
Stringham, Jack	1935–37
Stromberg, Doug	1977–79
Stroth, Vince	1980–82
Summers, Hyrum	1996–present
Sundwall, Pete	1956
Sutorius, Paul	1967–69
Swanson, Dave	1968–69
Swenson, Marc	1976–78
Swenson, Reed	1923–25
Tait, John	1996–present
Tanner, Kirk	1974
Tarleton, Vic	1992–93
Taylor, Clinton	1953–54
Taylor, Dan	1972–73
Taylor, Dan	1960–62
Taylor, Dave	1975–76
Taylor, Dunn	1923–24, '26
Taylor, Glen	1954, '56
Taylor, Golden	1934–35
Taylor, Jim	1956
Tennyson, Bob	1962–63
Terranova, Mark	1973, '75–76
Terry, Dave	1971–73
Thieman, Dick	1965–67
Thiel, Ted	1948
Thomas, Rodney	1984–87
Thompson, Pat	1986–88
Thompson, Tod	1976–78
Thorn, Paul	1928–30
Thorne, Dick	1925–27
Tiatia, Sim	1988, 90
Tibbetts, Ted	1941
Tibbitts, Ryan	1979–80
Tidwell, Dave	1983, 85
Tidwell, Neils	1979, '81–82
Tidwell, Randy	1978–79
Tingey, Kent	1978–79
Titensor, Glen	1979–80
Tiumalu, Casey	1982–83
Tolbert, Max	1949–51
Tooke, Dick	1949, '51
Toolson, Tom	1973–74
Toone, Cliff	1929, '31
Towle, Kevin	1985
Tree, Marion	1947–48
Tree, Ron	1970–72
Tripple, Leo	1963
Tucker, Glen	1932–33
Tucker, Larry	1974, '76
Tuipulotu, Peter	1987, '89–91
Tuipulotu, Tom	1983, 85
Tujague, Garrett	1990–91
Turley, Stan	1940
Ulufale, Mike	1994–95
Unger, Nick	1987
Unutoa, Morris	1989, '93–95
Uperesa, Keith	1974–77
Uselman, Mark	1974–75
Vacher, Clug	1929–30
Valdez, Nati	1989–92
Valgardson, Don	1976
Valgardson, Rich	1971
Van De Merwe, Jan	1976–77
VanDerWouden, John	1975–77
Van Leeuwen, Craig	1974
Van Leeuwen, Kent	1986
Van Valkenburg, Dan	1976
Van Valkenburg, Pete	1970–72
VanWoerkom, Scott	1989–90
Varner, Ross	1976–78
Varner, Stan	1973–75
Varoz, Brett	1983
Velasco, John	1953–54
Velasco, Ron	1976–78
Verbantz, Tom	1953–55
Verney, John	1934–35
Vest, Niles	1933
Vesterfelt, Jay	1962–63
VonColln, J. C.	1986–87
Vorwaller, Wes	1960
Wade, Alton	1953
Wadsworth, Jeff	1983
Waldo, Vern	1934–36
Walsh, John	1991, '93–94
Wakley, Ron	1967–69
Walker, Jason	1995–present
Walker, Kevin	1980–82
Walker, Mark	1979–81
Walter, John	1970
Wangsgard, Keith	1930–31
Wanosik, Bill	1963–65
Ward, Roy	1976
Wardell, Doug	1962–64
Warner, Max	1932
Warner, Meldon	1935, '37
Waters, Merrill	1936, '38
Watford, Dennis	1968–70
Watts, Stan	1936
Webb, Dennis	1978, 81
Webster, Gary	1985
Weed, Mark	1942
Weenig, Jay	1955–56
Weenig, John	1937, '39
Weenig, Val	1961–62
Weight, Gary	1974–75
Weinkauf, Mike	1967–69
Wells, Grant	1971–73
Wells, Von	1970–72
West, Henry	1952–54
Westover, Udel	1951–52
Wheat, Warren	1986–88
Wheeler, Melvin	1934–36
White, Brian	1986–88
White, Greg	1996–present
White, Leon	1982–85
Whitehead, Clark	1953
Whitney, Fred	1942
Whitsett, Vic	1979
Whittingham, Cary	1981, '83–85
Whittingham, Fred	1986–89
Whittingham, Kyle	1978–81
Wilcox, Jeff	1984–86
Wilgar, Dana	1973–76
Wilkes, Doug	1978–79
Wilkinson, Bob	1923
Wilkinson, Glen	1931
Willardson, Troy	1994
Willett, Ralph	1950
Williams, Doug	1978–79
Williams, Duaine	1992–93
Willis, Jamal	1991–94
Wilson, Grant	1964–66
Wilson, John	1962–63
Wilson, Marc	1977–79
Wilson, Pete	1931–33
Wilson, Rick	1988
Wilson, Rob	1978–80
Wilson, Ron	1970–71
Wing, George	1939–41
Wingard, Casey	1977–78
Witney, Frank	1946
Wong, Louis	1982–84
Wood, Dick	1961, '63–64
Wood, Don	1948, '52–53
Wood, John	1956
Wood, Rod	1976–78
Woodward, Jack	1934–35
Worthington, Vernal	1925–27
Wright, Bill	1960–62
Wright, Dave	1983–85
Wright, Frank	1934–35
Yancey, Daren	1995–present
Young, Ike	1922–23
Yarro, Justin	1992–93
Yarro, Roger	1960–61
Young, Jonathan	1982–83
Young, LeGrand	1959
Young, Mike	1987
Young, Steve	1981–83
Young, Tom	1992–94
Younger, Stan	1977–78
Zayas, Rich	1986–87
Zeller, Mike	1967–68
Zitting, Ron	1956
Zogg, Murray	1995–96
Zundel, Matt	1989–91
Zwahlen, Lynn	1972–73, '76–77

Bowl History

1974 Fiesta Bowl

December 28
Oklahoma State 16 Tempe, AZ
Brigham Young 6 Attendance 50,878

Scoring by Quarter	1	2	3	4	Final
Oklahoma State	0	7	3	6	16
Brigham Young	6	0	0	0	6

Team Statistics	OSU	BYU
Rushes-Yards	55-180	36-130
Passing Yards	77	181
Passes	7-18-0	15-31-3

Competing in its first post-season bowl game ever, BYU played Western Athletic Conference host to the Oklahoma State Cowboys.

The Cougars got off to a quick start with two field goals during the first quarter before All-WAC quarterback Gary Sheide suffered a dislocated shoulder in the last moments of the quarter. He was replaced by junior reserve Mark Giles.

The Cowboys took the scoring lead during the second quarter on a touchdown run around left end, giving Oklahoma State a 7–6 halftime advantage.

OSU regained possession of the ball on the Cougars' 17-yard line after intercepting Giles, but the Cowboys were unable to convert on the turnover.

A field goal from 32 yards out put the Cowboys in front 10–7 at the end of the third quarter. With 1:14 remaining in the game, Oklahoma State scored another touchdown on a 40-yard halfback pass to complete the scoring.

The Cougars out-gained Oklahoma State in total yardage, 301–214. Giles was 11 of 26 for 138 yards. After three losses and a tie to open the season, the Cougars reeled off seven straight victories prior to the bowl game.

1976 Tangerine Bowl

December 18
Oklahoma State 49 Orlando, FL
Brigham Young 21 Attendance 37,812

Scoring by Quarter	1	2	3	4	Final
Oklahoma State	7	21	21	0	49
Brigham Young	0	14	7	0	21

Team Statistics	OSU	BYU
Rushes-Yards	70-375	26-46
Passing Yards	27	209
Passes	2-10-0	23-34-4

Powerful Oklahoma State, sparked by All-American Terry Miller (173 yards rushing on 23 carries), used four pass interceptions and a fumble recovery to capture the 31st annual Tangerine Bowl contest. Defensively, the Cowboys yielded only 46 yards rushing.

The Cougars, however, stayed close in the first half, which ended 28–14. But Dave Lowry returned the second-half kickoff 102 yards (a Tangerine Bowl record) to move the Cougars to within seven at 28–21. From there, it was all Cowboys.

BYU's Gifford Nielsen completed 23 of 34 passes for 209 yards and one touchdown, but the Cougars could only roll up 255 yards to Oklahoma State's 402.

BYU entered the game with a 9–2 record, while Oklahoma State came in after tying for the Big 8 title. The Cowboys missed out on the Orange Bowl because of the conference tie-breaking formula.

Later, the stadium was expanded and the name changed to the Florida Citrus Bowl.

1978 Holiday Bowl

December 22
Navy 23 San Diego, CA
Brigham Young 16 Attendance 52,500

Scoring by Quarter	1	2	3	4	Final
Navy	0	3	7	13	23
Brigham Young	3	6	7	0	16

Team Statistics	Navy	BYU
Rushes-Yards	58-214	33-74
Passing Yards	138	181
Passes	8-14-1	16-34-2

The inaugural Holiday Bowl pitted two teams with local drawing power, the Naval Academy and Brigham Young University. Despite chilly temperatures, the two teams engaged in a hard-hitting battle.

Defense dominated the first two quarters. Brent Johnson put the Cougars on the scoreboard first with a 33-yard field goal with 8:26 left in the first quarter. But Navy's Bob Tata boomed a 40-yard field goal to tie the score at 3–3.

Jim McMahon sent the Cougars ahead with a 10-yard pass to Mike Chronister, but Johnson missed the PAT. McMahon ran another in from two yards out in the third period for a 16–3 BYU lead.

Navy cut the lead to 16–10 after three quarters and then tied the game on two field goals in the fourth quarter, but it was a 65-yard pass to Phil McConkey that did the Cougars in.

McConkey was named Best Offensive Player and BYU's Tom Enlow won Best Defensive Player honors. Navy finished the year at 9–3, BYU at 9–4.

The 1979 season ended with BYU leading the nation in scoring, passing and total offense. At 11–0, the Cougars were one of the few undefeated, untied teams in the nation.

Those kinds of credentials, along with its No. 9 national ranking in the UPI and AP polls made BYU the favorite over the at-large entry, Indiana.

The opportunistic Hoosiers played the Cougars tough, holding a 21–17 lead at the half.

BYU jumped ahead in the third quarter, 24–21, on a 13-yard pass from All-American Marc Wilson to Homer Jones. The Cougars fell behind, 31–24, but regained the lead at 34–31 on a 15-yard pass to Eric Lane. With 12:14 left to play, BYU padded the lead on the third field goal of the game by Brent Johnson.

But midway through the fourth quarter, Indiana's Tim Wilbur returned a punt 62 yards to push the Hoosiers ahead 38–37.

With 2:06 remaining, the Cougars moved the ball 69 yards to the Indiana 10. Then, with 11 seconds left, Johnson missed a 27-yard field goal that would have won the game. Wilson was voted the MVP on offense (28 of 43 for 380 yards) and Indiana's Wilbur won the honor for defense.

Clay Brown caught nine passes for 142 yards. Lane grabbed nine passes for 79 yards and also scored a rushing touchdown. Jones scored a touchdown and had 126 yards on seven kickoff returns.

1979 Holiday Bowl

December 21
Indiana 38 — **San Diego, CA**
Brigham Young 37 — **Attendance 52,200**

Scoring by Quarter	1	2	3	4	Final
Indiana	14	7	10	7	38
Brigham Young	14	3	17	3	37

Team Statistics	Indiana	BYU
Rushes-Yards	59-183	30-140
Passing Yards	171	380
Passes	11-30-1	28-43-3

One observer said the 1980 Holiday Bowl was actually two ball games—a contest which lasted most of four quarters and another of four minutes duration.

SMU controlled the "first game," leaving the Cougars behind 20 points with only minutes remaining. Unfortunately, many fans either turned off their TV sets or left the stadium in San Diego before the "second game" began. In the final four minutes, BYU surged to a stunning 46–45 win.

For 56 minutes the Mustangs taught the Cougars a lesson in running the football. The Mustangs' two great running backs, Craig James and Eric Dickerson, rushed for a combined total of 335 yards.

With 4:07 remaining in the game, SMU scored to go ahead, 45–25. From there the Cougars connected on a TD pass, recovered an on-side kick, scored on a one-yard run by Scott Phillips, blocked a punt. Finally, with three seconds left on the clock, Jim McMahon connected on a "Hail Mary" pass of 41 yards to Clay Brown. With the score tied, Kurt Gunther kicked the extra point to send BYU fans streaming onto the field.

McMahon was 32 of 49 passes for 446 yards. It may have been the most exciting bowl game ever with the Cougars getting 21 points in the final 2:33.

1980 Holiday Bowl

December 21
Brigham Young 46 — **San Diego, CA**
Southern Methodist 45 — **Attend: 52,214**

Scoring by Quarter	1	2	3	4	Final
Brigham Young	7	6	6	27	46
SMU	19	10	9	7	45

Team Statistics	SMU	BYU
Rushes-Yards	66-393	24-(-2)
Passing Yards	53	446
Passes	6-11-0	32-49-1

The 1981 edition of the Holiday Bowl fit the mold of its predecessors. This time it was the Cougars of BYU versus the Cougars of Washington State.

BYU held a 24-7 lead at halftime, then pushed the score to 31–7 as Tom Holmoe intercepted a pass and returned it 35 yards to give the WAC champions a comfortable edge.

As the second half progressed, it appeared BYU would be the come-from-behind victim in this one. With only 59 seconds left in the third quarter, Washington State scored to make it 31–28. But Jim McMahon took over moving BYU 82 yards for a score to stretch the lead to 38–28.

Statistically, it was a typical McMahon game, 27 of 43 with no interceptions and three touchdowns. Tight end Gordon Hudson had an excellent game, collecting seven catches for 126 yards and a touchdown. Dan Plater also caught a touchdown pass and Waymon Hamilton scored on the ground.

Washington State quarterbacks Clete Casper and Ricky Turner completed only eight passes for 106 yards but Turner had 82 yards rushing while Don LaBomme had 79.

Each team scored five touchdowns, so the difference actually came midway through the second quarter when Kurt Gunther connected on a 20-yard field goal after a BYU drive stalled on the Washington State three.

1981 Holiday Bowl

December 18
Brigham Young 38 — **San Diego, CA**
Washington State 36 — **Attend: 52,419**

Scoring by Quarter	1	2	3	4	Final
Brigham Young	7	17	7	7	38
Washington St.	0	7	21	8	36

Team Statistics	Wash. St.	BYU
Rushes-Yards	53-245	32-69
Passing Yards	106	368
Passes	8-25-2	28-44-0

1982 Holiday Bowl

December 17
Ohio State 47 — San Diego, CA
Brigham Young 17 — Attendance 52,533

Scoring by Quarter	1	2	3	4	Final
Ohio State	3	14	17	13	47
Brigham Young	0	10	0	7	17

Team Statistics	Ohio State	BYU
Rushes-Yards	66-329	18-60
Passing Yards	132	352
Passes	11-19-0	28-46-1

The Cougars had their two-game Holiday Bowl win streak snapped by Ohio State, 47–17.

BYU's bubble burst at the outset of the third quarter, when the Buckeyes reeled off 17 unanswered points. Tim Spencer blew through the Cougar defense for 167 yards, including a record-setting 61-yard touchdown run in the second quarter that put Ohio State up, 10–7.

Steve Young completed 27 of 45 passes for 341 yards, but BYU had a tough time getting into the end zone. The Cougars turned the ball over to Ohio State three times inside the 30 and saw the Buckeyes convert each turnover into a score.

The Cougars took the lead early in the second quarter with a seven-yard strike to Neil Balholm. But Spencer's long gallop and a blocked punt put the Buckeyes up, 17–10, at halftime.

Big fullback Vaughn Broadnax scored on the opening drive of the second half, and on the next play, Young was intercepted and Spencer ran 18 yards to put Ohio State in control for good.

BYU's only other score came midway through the fourth quarter when Gordon Hudson caught a 13-yard pass. Ohio State quarterback Mike Tomczak had only 132 yards passing and no touchdowns, but his fleet of running backs scored six times on the ground.

Ten different BYU players caught passes, led by Hudson (see photo) with seven receptions for 81 yards and Balholm with 58 yards receiving.

1983 Holiday Bowl

December 23
Brigham Young 21 — San Diego, CA
Missouri 17 — Attendance 51,480

Scoring by Quarter	1	2	3	4	Final
Brigham Young	0	7	7	7	21
Missouri	7	3	0	7	17

Team Statistics	Missouri	BYU
Rushes-Yards	64-252	25-42
Passing Yards	86	328
Passes	7-16-2	25-37-3

Yet another chapter was added to the saga of impossible, thrilling Holiday Bowl finishes when BYU defeated Missouri, 21–17.

The game was billed as a classic matchup between Missouri's stubborn defense and BYU's explosive offense, led by quarterback Steve Young.

Missouri held BYU to just 167 yards and seven points in the first half, while BYU's defense allowed the Tigers only 157 yards and 10 points. Missouri got its first-half points on a two-yard run by Eric Drain and a 37-yard field goal by Brad Burditt.

BYU's touchdown came on a 10-yard quarterback draw by Young. In the second half, Young hit Eddie Stinnett with a 33-yard touchdown pass. But Missouri came right back with another two-yard plunge by Drain.

A valiant goal-line stand by BYU gave the Cougars the ball on the six-yard-line with 3:57 left in the game. Led by Young, the Cougars moved down the field to the Missouri 15 with under a minute to play. On first-and-10 at the Tigers' 15, Young handed to Stinnett, who faked a sweep right and threw back across the field to Young.

The Stinnett pass barely cleared the outstretched hands of Missouri's Bobby Bell allowing Young to gather it in and ramble 15 yards to the end zone. The PAT gave BYU a 21–17 lead with 23 seconds left.

Kyle Morrell intercepted a Missouri desperation pass at the BYU 2-yard line and returned it to the 17 to seal the win. The win gave BYU four bowl victories in five years between 1980–84.

1984 Holiday Bowl

December 21
Brigham Young 24 — San Diego, CA
Michigan 17 — Attendance 61,243

Scoring by Quarter	1	2	3	4	Final
Brigham Young	0	10	0	14	24
Michigan	0	7	7	3	17

Team Statistics	Michigan	BYU
Rushes-Yards	49-120	27-112
Passing Yards	82	371
Passes	7-15-1	35-49-3

Holiday Bowl VII lived up to all the glamour and excitement of the previous six bowls, plus it had a new dimension—national championship luster—thanks to BYU's undefeated, untied season and No. 1 ranking. The 24–17 Cougar victory marked the first time in years that a non-New Year's Day bowl game determined the national championship. After a scoreless first quarter in which Cougar quarterback Robbie Bosco was forced to the sideline with an injured knee and ankle, the game began to develop drama.

BYU scored first with 8:37 left in the first half on a five-yard run by Kelly Smith. The touchdown was set up when a limping Bosco returned to the lineup and engineered an 80-yard drive.

The Wolverines responded by putting together an 80-yard scoring drive of their own, culminating on Rick Rogers' five-yard touchdown run up the middle. The PAT tied the score at seven. The tie was short-lived however, as a 31-yard field goal by Lee Johnson with time running out in the first half gave BYU a 10–7 lead at the break.

Midway through the third period, Michigan went on top for the first time at 14–10 on a 10-yard scoring strike from Bob Zurbrugg to Bob Perryman. The Wolverines added to their lead when Bob Bergeron nailed a 32-yard field goal to make the Michigan lead 17–10 with 14:14 to play. The Cougar offense then produced an 80-yard drive that culminated with a seven-yard Bosco-to-Glen Kozlowski touchdown pass to tie the game at 17 with 10:51 to go. Bosco's 13-yard scoring toss to Smith with 1:23 remaining made it 24–17. Two plays later Marv Allen intercepted a pass to clinch a 13–0 season and the Cougars' first-ever national championship.

1985 Florida Citrus Bowl

December 28
Ohio State 10 — **Orlando, FL**
Brigham Young 7 — **Attendance 50,920**

Scoring by Quarter	1	2	3	4	Final
Ohio State	0	3	7	0	10
Brigham Young	0	7	0	0	7

Team Statistics	Ohio State	BYU
Rushes-Yards	42-133	22-88
Passing Yards	196	261
Passes	19-36-0	26-50-4

In what promised to be an offensive showdown between pass-happy BYU (11–2) and rough and tumble Ohio State (8–3), two of the nation's top defenses took center stage. In fact, the game's only touchdowns were produced by a noseguard on an interception and a reserve wide receiver on a broken play.

Buckeye kicker Rich Spangler tallied the first points of the game with a 47-yard field goal early in the second quarter to give Ohio State a 3–0 lead. BYU attempted to answer with a long drive of its own, only to come away empty after Vai Sikahema fumbled on an apparent touchdown plunge.

Before the first half ended, quarterback Robbie Bosco rolled left, whirled right and found wide receiver David Miles on a 38-yard strike to give the Cougars a 7–3 halftime lead.

In the second half, Ohio State noseguard Larry Kolic intercepted Bosco and took it in for a touchdown to give the Buckeyes a 10–7 lead.

Leon White and Kyle Whittingham recovered fumbles but Kolic got another interception and Terry White intercepted two in the end zone to stop BYU threats—one with 3:38 to play and again with three seconds left.

Ohio State was the benefactor of six Cougar turnovers, and the Buckeyes went home the victor. Matt Bellini had 89 yards receiving while Lakei Heimuli added 10 receptions for 77 yards.

1986 Freedom Bowl

December 30
UCLA 31 — **Anaheim, CA**
Brigham Young 10 — **Attendance 55,422**

Scoring by Quarter	1	2	3	4	Final
UCLA	7	0	17	7	31
Brigham Young	3	0	0	7	10

Team Statistics	UCLA	BYU
Rushes-Yards	49-423	43-73
Passing Yards	95	221
Passes	8-21-1	25-43-3

Although BYU failed to win the WAC title, the Cougars kept alive an impressive streak of nine bowl appearances in a row by being invited to the third annual Freedom Bowl. There they met familiar foe UCLA. The two teams had met in 1985 when the Bruins came from behind to win a tough game in Provo, 27–24.

The Freedom Bowl, however, proved different as UCLA outstanding running back Gaston Green broke open a close game in the third quarter as the Bruins went on to win 31–10. Green finished with 266 yards on 33 carries.

The first half was all defensive as the two teams punted nine times in the first 30 minutes. BYU struck first when linebacker Andy Katoa recovered a UCLA fumble at the Bruin 47 and Leonard Chitty put the Cougars ahead 3–0 with a 32-yard field goal.

UCLA stormed ahead to stay with a 71-yard touchdown drive highlighted by a 49-yard run on a reverse by Bruin receiver Karl Dorrell.From then on, it was UCLA most of the way. Cougar quarterbacks Bob Jensen and Mike Young managed to pass for over 200 yards, but UCLA and Green did most of the damage.

Costly injuries to standouts Mark Bellini and Katoa hindered the Cougar effort, but Outland Trophy winner Jason Buck turned in another strong effort.

1987 All American Bowl

December 22
Virginia 22 — **Birmingham, AL**
Brigham Young 16 — **Attendance 37,000**

Scoring by Quarter	1	2	3	4	Final
Virginia	7	7	0	8	22
Brigham Young	3	0	6	7	16

Team Statistics	Virginia	BYU
Rushes-Yards	43-187	26-95
Passing Yards	162	394
Passes	10-19-2	37-61-1

The 11th annual All American Bowl began with temperatures in the 40s and BYU never warmed up. The Cougars' 10th consecutive bowl appearance included several records, but BYU lost 22–16 in its first-ever meeting with Virginia. Sean Covey attempted 61 passes, David Miles had 188 yards in receptions and Pat Thompson only punted once, but BYU fell short several times.

Darren Handley, BYU's leading receiver, dropped a touchdown pass in the first quarter before BYU settled for a 20-yard field goal by Leonard Chitty. However, Chitty, who set a season mark for field goals (18) and consecutive PATs (29), missed from 51 and 47 yards as Virginia took a 14–3 lead into the intermission.

BYU got to the Virginia two-yard-line midway through the third quarter only to have a fourth-down pass tipped away. Later, Freddie Whittingham scampered eight yards to cut the lead to 14–9 at the end of the third quarter.

Virginia, led by quarterback Scott Secules, the game's MVP, made a crucial 76-yard drive to go ahead 22–9 with 11 minutes left. Then, BYU went the same distance to score on a one-yard pass to Whittingham with seven minutes remaining.

But that was a close as the Cougars would get.

Ironically, nine years earlier on the same date Virginia Coach George Welsh led Navy to a 23–16 win over BYU in the inaugural Holiday Bowl.

1988 Freedom Bowl

December 29
Brigham Young 20 — Anaheim, CA
Colorado 17 — Attendance 35,941

Scoring by Quarter	1	2	3	4	Final
Brigham Young	7	0	7	6	20
Colorado	7	7	0	3	17

Team Statistics	Colorado	BYU
Rushes-Yards	60-273	42-154
Passing Yards	64	168
Passes	5-16-2	15-28-1

A star was born in the fifth annual Freedom Bowl when Ty Detmer came off the bench to earn MVP honors while leading the Cougars to an upset victory over Colorado.

Cool weather didn't hamper diminutive Eric Bieniemy, who rushed 33 times for 144 yards and two touchdowns. But his heroics couldn't offset Detmer's 11 for 19 and 129 yards in the second half. Scott Peterson made an interception to set up the game-winning field goal.

It was an exciting contest for the 35,941 fans (49,694 tickets were sold) in attendance. A fumble at midfield led to the Buffaloes' first score and then Sean Covey found Mike Salido to tie the score. An interception in the end zone stopped a BYU drive early in the second quarter as the Cougars trailed at the half, 14–7.

A Detmer to Chuck Cutler pass tied the game in the third quarter but Colorado took a 17–14 lead early in the final quarter.

BYU then moved from its own four to the Buffalo 14 and tied the game with 4:11 left on a 31-yarder by Chaffetz. Three plays later, Peterson's interception and a 15-yard penalty put the ball at the Colorado 32. With 2:33 left, Chaffetz booted a 35-yarder for the victory.

Halfback Matt Bellini carried eight times for 78 yards and caught four passes for 41 yards.

1989 Holiday Bowl

December 29
Penn State 50 — San Diego, CA
Brigham Young 39 — Attendance 61,113

Scoring by Quarter	1	2	3	4	Final
Penn State	3	9	17	21	50
Brigham Young	3	10	13	13	39

Team Statistics	Penn State	BYU
Rushes-Yards	54-249	23-75
Passing Yards	215	576
Passes	11-21-1	42-59-2

Two unusual plays late in the game kept BYU from downing Penn State and offset 576 yards passing by Ty Detmer—the highest total ever in a bowl game.

For his effort, and thanks to blocking from Outland Trophy winner Mohammed Elewonibi, Detmer had the rare privilege of sharing MVP honors despite playing on the losing team.

The other co-MVP was the Nittany Lions' Blair Thomas, who rushed for 186 yards.

BYU, which trailed 41–26 with nine and a half minutes remaining, scored twice to cut the lead to 41–39 with 2:30 to play. The Cougars went for a two-point conversion to tie the game, but Detmer's pass was intercepted in the end zone by Penn State linebacker Andre Collins and returned 102 yards for two points.

Down 43–39, the Cougars, led by Bob Davis, forced the Lions to punt , giving BYU the ball on its own 12 with two minutes left. Passes to Brent Nyberg, Matt Bellini, Chris Smith and Andy Boyce moved the ball to the Penn State 38 with a minute left to play.

Then, what appeared to be a sack by Penn State safety Gary Brown turned into a score for the Nittany Lions. Brown stripped the ball from Detmer at the Penn State 47 and raced 53 yards for the touchdown.

Bellini had 10 catches for 124 yards while Boyce had 127 yards in receptions and Nyberg 117.

Penn State finished the season ranked 14th by UPI and 15th by AP and CNN/USA Today. BYU was 18th in the UPI poll and 22nd in the others.

1990 Holiday Bowl

December 29
Texas A&M 65 — San Diego, CA
Brigham Young 14 — Attendance 61,441

Scoring by Quarter	1	2	3	4	Final
Texas A&M	14	23	7	21	65
Brigham Young	7	0	7	0	14

Team Statistics	Texas A&M	BYU
Rushes-Yards	64-356	21-(-12)
Passing Yards	324	197
Passes	16-18-0	15-32-1

Led by quarterback Bucky Richardson and All-America running back Darren Lewis, underdog Texas A&M was out to show it belonged among the nation's elite.

The Cougars entered the game beat up. Defensive backs Tony Crutchfield and Norm Dixon weren't able to suit up and Heisman Trophy winner Ty Detmer was playing with a slight separation in his non-throwing shoulder.

The second largest Holiday Bowl crowd ever (61,441) watched the Aggies march 80 yards in 13 plays to take a 7–0 lead. The Cougars tied the score on an eight-yard Detmer-to-Chris Smith touchdown pass, but after that, the game was all Texas A&M. The Aggies went on to score 23 points in the second quarter enroute to a 37–7 halftime lead.

With the game out of hand, the big story was William Thomas' crunching sack that separated Detmer's throwing shoulder and put him out of the game early in the third quarter.

The Aggies continued to dominate by racking up nearly 200 yards rushing in the second half. Texas A&M's Richardson would go on to be named Offensive Player of the Game by piling up 344 yards in total offense. Thomas was named the top defensive player.

BYU finished the season ranked 17th by UPI, 20th by CNN/USA Today and 22nd by AP. BYU had been as high as fourth prior to its first loss.

A tipped pass that was picked off in the end zone with less than 30 seconds remaining stifled BYU's hopes of knocking off seventh-ranked Iowa in the 14th annual Holiday Bowl. Ty Detmer turned in another great performance in his last appearance as a Cougar, passing for 350 yards and two touchdowns against a team that led the Big 10 in defense and sacks.

Quarterback Matt Rodgers led Iowa on a 74-yards scoring march on the game's opening drive. The Hawkeyes also scored on another long drive in the second quarter.

Down 13–0, BYU finally got things rolling. Starting on the BYU 22, Detmer connected on five of six passes to move the Cougars to the Iowa nine. From there, he found fullback Peter Tuipulotu for the touchdown. The PAT failed and the halftime score was 13–6.

BYU opened the fourth with an 87-yard drive that culminated with a Detmer-to-Tyler Anderson touchdown from 29 yards out. Earl Kauffman connected on the PAT to tie the score at 13.

Each team threatened to score late in the fourth quarter. Iowa missed a 40-yard field goal with 4:19 left.

On the game's final drive the Cougars move inside the Iowa 20 with 33 seconds left to play, but Detmer's pass to tight end Byron Rex was tipped and picked off by Hawkeye safety Carlos James in the end zone to preserve the tie.

Josh Arnold of BYU earned defensive MVP honors as BYU finished the season ranked 23rd in the AP and CNN/USA Today polls. Iowa was 10th in both polls.

1991 Holiday Bowl

December 30
Brigham Young 13 — **San Diego, CA**
Iowa 13 — **Attendance 60,646**

Scoring by Quarter	1	2	3	4	Final
Brigham Young	0	6	0	7	13
Iowa	6	7	0	0	13

Team Statistics	Iowa	BYU
Rushes-Yards	33-125	33-80
Passing Yards	221	350
Passes	19-28-1	29-44-1

Kansas kicker Dan Eichloff booted a 48-yard field goal with 2:57 left to play, giving the Jayhawks a victory over BYU, the WAC tri-champion.

Tom Young, who completed 15 of 31 passes for 262 yards in his first varsity start, was named Most Valuable Player for BYU. Tackle Dana Stubblefield, who had three of the six sacks on Young, won the honor for Kansas.

Young had been pressed into action when Ryan Hancock suffered knee ligament damage against Utah in the final regular-season game.

The Cougars took an early lead when Hema Heimuli scrambled 94 yards on the open kick off for a score. Kansas tied the game two plays later when wide receiver Matt Gay threw a 74-yard touchdown pass to tight end Rodney Harris.

BYU took a 14–9 lead in the second quarter when Jamal Willis ran 29 yards for a score. Eichloff then cut the halftime score to 14–12 with a 42-yard field goal.

But the kicking game would prove the downfall as the Cougars missed a 36-yard field goal in the first quarter as well as a 31-yarder and misplayed an extra point attempt in the third quarter.

Young threw 10 yards to Otis Sterling for the only score of the third quarter. Kansas quarterback Chip Hilleary then tied the game by directing a 75-yard drive in a minute and a half, scoring the touchdown and then running for a two-point conversion.

1992 Aloha Bowl

December 25
Kansas 23 — **Honolulu, HI**
Brigham Young 20 — **Attendance 42,933**

Scoring by Quarter	1	2	3	4	Final
Kansas	9	3	0	11	23
Brigham Young	7	7	6	0	20

Team Statistics	Kansas	BYU
Rushes-Yards	49-172	32-56
Passing Yards	200	262
Passes	12-24-0	15-31-1

The Cougars took Big 10 Co-Champion Ohio State to the wire at the 16th annual Thrifty Car Rental Holiday Bowl and came up just short.

BYU had four downs and 32 seconds to tie or win the game from the OSU six-yard line, but four straight John Walsh passes into the end zone fell to the ground and OSU slipped away with the win.

BYU got to the Ohio State six, 14, 22-yard lines in the second half without scoring. Meanwhile, Raymont Harris, OSU's senior halfback, battered the BYU defense all night long, scoring three touchdowns on his way to a record 235 yards rushing.

Despite Harris' rushing, the Cougars managed to go to the halftime break tied at 21. Jamal Willis and Bryce Doman each collected 27-yard Walsh offerings and walk-on tight end Chad Lewis made a spectacular one-handed touchdown grab in the corner of the end zone to bail the Cougars out of a fourth-and-eight situation.

After Harris' short touchdown run late in the third, BYU and OSU traded possessions until late into the fourth quarter. After forcing a rare Buckeye punt, BYU got the ball back on its own 42 with 43 seconds left.

On first down, Walsh hooked up with senior co-captain Eric Drage who ran away from Buckeye defenders and advanced the ball 52 yards to the OSU six-yard-line.

Walsh had 389 yards and fullback Kalin Hall rushed for 42 yards on 11 carries. Tyler Anderson returned five kicks for 145 yards, including an exciting 45-yarder. Harris and Walsh shared MVP honors.

1993 Holiday Bowl

December 30
Ohio State 28 — **San Diego, CA**
Brigham Young 21 — **Attendance 52,108**

Scoring by Quarter	1	2	3	4	Final
Ohio State	14	7	7	0	28
Brigham Young	7	14	0	0	21

Team Statistics	Ohio State	BYU
Rushes-Yards	56-330	26-50
Passing Yards	61	389
Passes	6-13-0	25-44-1

1994 Copper Bowl

December 29
Brigham Young 31 — **Tucson, AZ**
Oklahoma 6 — **Attendance 45,122**

Scoring by Quarter	1	2	3	4	Final
Brigham Young	7	10	7	7	31
Oklahoma	0	0	0	6	6

Team Statistics	Oklahoma	BYU
Rushes-Yards	33-72	33-71
Passing Yards	163	485
Passes	13-30-1	32-46-0

BYU fans celebrated the New Year early as the Cougars dominated Oklahoma and ended its five-year winning drought in bowl games.

Quarterback John Walsh and the offense clicked on all cylinders and the Cougars' defense was dominating throughout the ESPN telecast.

Walsh threw a seven-yard TD pass to Bryce Doman in the first quarter and had a 25-yard pass to Mike Johnston in the second quarter.

A four-yard scoring pass to Johnston in the third quarter and a 28-yard touchdown pass to Doman in the fourth quarter vaulted Walsh's stats to 454 yards and four touchdowns on 31 of 45 passes with no interceptions against the Sooner defense which had held national champion Nebraska to 13 points.

BYU's defense was dominating as it held Oklahoma to just 72 yards rushing and 163 yards passing—most of those in the last quarter. The Sooners did not cross midfield until their ninth possession on the second-to-last play of the third quarter.

Jamal Willis caught seven passes for 103 yards and was chosen Offensive Player of the Game. Walsh was named MVP in what would be his final game at BYU.

Guard Evan Pilgrim earned second-team All-America honors and played in the Hula Bowl along with defensive end Travis Hall. Willis and defensive end Randy Brock played in the East-West Shrine Game.

BYU finished 10th in the CNN/USA Today poll and 18th in the Associated Press poll.

1996 Cotton Bowl

January 1, 1997
Brigham Young 19 — **Dallas, TX**
Kansas State 15 — **Attendance 71,928**

Scoring by Quarter	1	2	3	4	Final
Brigham Young	5	0	0	14	19
Kansas State	0	8	7	0	15

Team Statistics	Kansas State	BYU
Rushes-Yards	32-86	36-114
Passing Yards	233	291
Passes	14-28-2	21-36-1

BYU assumed the nation's longest winning streak with a come-from-behind 19–15 victory in the 61st annual Cotton Bowl. It was the first New Year's Day appearance for both 14th-ranked Kansas State and fifth-ranked BYU.

More than 40,000-purple clad Kansas State supporters out-numbered the 10,000 Cougar patrons as 71,928 fans filled the Cotton Bowl. Paul James returned to the Cougar radio microphone after a game's absence due to six bypasses in heart surgery, and BYU fullback Mark Atuaia became a father the day before kickoff.

BYU got on the board first with a safety, then turned the ensuing punt into a field goal to lead 5–0 in the first quarter. The safety came when linebacker Shay Muirbrook, the game's defensive MVP, collected one of his six sacks. Kansas State took a half-time lead with a 41-yard Hail Mary pass and a successful two-point conversion with no time left on the clock.

The Wildcats increased the lead to 15–5 in the third quarter when offensive co-MVP Kevin Lockett caught a 72-yard TD. Fueled by consecutive controversial interference no-calls and continual trash-talking by KSU, quarterback Steve Sarkisian engineered two fourth-quarter drives capped by touchdown passes of 32-yards to James Dye and 28-yards to K.O. Kealaluhi. Sarkisian, an offensive co-MVP, completed 21 passes to tie a Cotton Bowl record held by Roger Staubach of Navy.

KSU drove the length of the field before Cougar cornerback Omarr Morgan juggled an interception from a Wildcat slant pattern at the 12 yardline to secure the game.

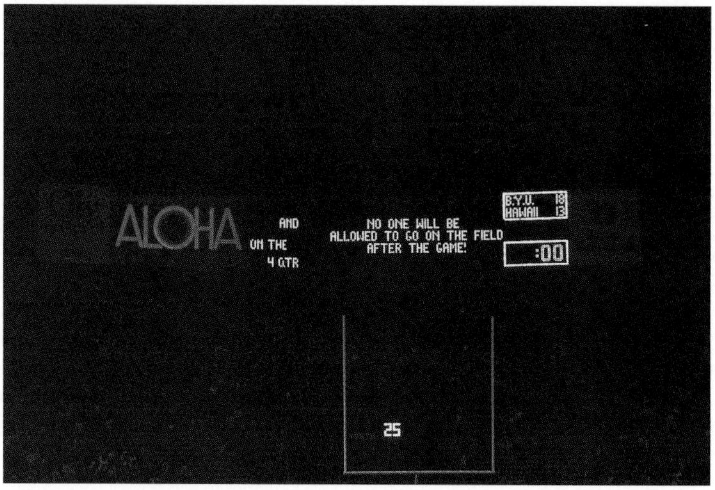

BYU and NCAA Bowl Records

INDIVIDUAL

Most Total Yards: 594, Ty Detmer, BYU vs. Penn State, Holiday Bowl 1989 (576 passing yards, 67 plays)
Most Passing Attempts: 61, Sean Covey, BYU vs. Virginia, All American Bowl 1987
Most Completions: 42, Ty Detmer, BYU vs. Penn State, Holiday Bowl 1989
Net Passing Yards: 576, Ty Detmer, BYU vs. Penn State, Holiday Bowl 1989 (42 of 59 with two interceptions)
Most Kickoff Returns: 7, Homer Jones, BYU vs. Indiana, Holiday Bowl 1979
Most Extra-Point Kick Attempts: 9, Layne Talbot, Texas A&M vs. BYU, Holiday Bowl 1990
Most Extra-Point Kicks Made: 9, Layne Talbot, Texas A&M vs. BYU, Holiday Bowl 1990
Most Tackles Made for losses: 5, Michael Jones, Colorado vs. BYU, Freedom Bowl 1988
Most Quarterback Sacks: 4, Bobby Bell, Missouri vs. BYU, Holiday Bowl 1983

TEAM

Highest Rushing Average (Min. 30 attempts): 8.6 UCLA vs. BYU, Freedom Bowl 1986
Most Passing Yards: 576, BYU vs. Penn State, 1989 Holiday Bowl
Most Touchdowns: 9, Texas A&M vs. BYU, Holiday Bowl 1990
Most Points, Winning Team: 65, Texas A&M vs. BYU, Holiday Bowl 1990
Most Points, Losing Team: 45, Southern Methodist vs. BYU, Holiday Bowl 1980
Most Points, Both Teams: 91, BYU vs. Southern Methodist, Holiday Bowl 1980
Most Points Scored in Second Half Both Teams: 64, Penn State (38) vs. BYU (26), Holiday Bowl 1989
Most Points Scored in 1st Quarter, Both Teams: 28, Indiana (14) vs. BYU (14), Holiday Bowl 1979
Most First Downs, Both teams: 61, BYU (35) vs. Penn State (26), Holiday Bowl 1989
Most First Downs Passing: 27, BYU vs. Penn State, Holiday Bowl 1989

Consecutive Bowls

School	Cons.	Total
1. Nebraska	27	35
2. Alabama	26	49
3. Michigan	21	27
4. BYU	17	20
5. Ohio State	15	29

BYU vs. Conferences

vs. Big 10	1-4-1
vs. Big 8	3-3
vs. Big 12	1-0
vs. Pac-10	1-1
vs. SWC	1-1
vs. ACC	0-1
vs. Independents	0-2

BYU's All-Time Bowl Results

Year	Opponent	Conference	Bowl	W/L	Score
1974	Oklahoma State	Big Eight	Fiesta	L	16-6
1976	Oklahoma State	Big Eight	Tangerine	L	49-21
1978	Navy	Independent	Holiday	L	23-16
1979	Indiana	Big 10	Holiday	L	38-37
1980	SMU	Southwest	Holiday	W	46-45
1981	Washington State	Pac-10	Holiday	W	38-36
1982	Ohio State	Big 10	Holiday	L	47-17
1983	Missouri	Big Eight	Holiday	W	21-17
1984	Michigan	Big 10	Holiday	W	24-17
1985	Ohio State	Big 10	Citrus	L	10-7
1986	UCLA	Pac-10	Freedom	L	31-10
1987	Virginia	Atlantic Coast	All American	L	22-16
1988	Colorado	Big Eight	Freedom	W	20-17
1989	Penn State	Independent	Holiday	L	50-39
1990	Texas A&M	Southwest	Holliday	L	65-14
1991	Iowa	Big 10	Holiday	T	13-13
1992	Kansas	Big Eight	Aloha	L	23-20
1993	Ohio State	Big 10	Holiday	L	28-21
1994	Oklahoma	Big Eight	Copper	W	31-6
1996	Kansas St.	Big 12	Cotton	W	19-15

BYU's combined record going into bowl games: 188-49-2 (.791)
Opponent's combined record going into bowl games: 153-64-4 (.701)

Individual Records

SCORING

Most Touchdowns Scored

Game	5	Eric Lane vs. Utah State, 10/13/79
Season	16	Waymon Hamilton, 1981
Career	40	Jamal Willis, 1991-94

Most Touchdowns Responsible For

Game	8	Marc Wilson vs. Colorado State, 10/15/77
	8	Jim McMahon vs. Utah State, 10/18/80
Season	53	Jim McMahon, 1980
Career	135	Ty Detmer, 1988-91#

Most Points Scored

Game	30	Eric Lane vs. Utah State, 10/13/79
Season	96	Waymon Hamilton, 1981
Career	243	Kurt Gunther, 1980-82

Most PATs Attempted

Game	10	Kurt Gunther vs. UTEP, 11/1/80
	10	Jason Chaffetz vs. Utah, 11/18/89
Season	71	Kurt Gunther, 1980#
Career	179	Kurt Gunther, 1980-82#

Most PATs Made

Game	10	Jason Chaffetz vs. Utah, 11/18/89
Season	64	Kurt Gunther, 1980
Career	162	Kurt Gunther, 1980-82

Most Consecutive PATs Made

Game	10	Jason Chaffetz vs. Utah 11/18/89
Season	61	Ethan Pochman, 1996
Career	61	Ethan Pochman, 1996

Most Points Kicking

Game	16	Ethan Pochman vs. Arkansas State, 8/31/96
	16	Joe Liljenquist vs. Colorado State, 9/20/69
Season	123	Ethan Pochman, 1996
Career	243	Kurt Gunther (1980-82)

Most Field Goals Made

Game	5	Joe Liljenquist vs. Colorado State, 9/20/69
Season	20	Ethan Pochman, 1996
Career	34	Leonard Chitty (1986-87)
Longest	53	Dennis Patera vs. USU, 1967

RUSHING

Most Yards

Game	272	Eldon Fortie vs. George Washington, 9/29/62
Season	1,386	Pete Van Valkenburg, 1972
Career	2,970	Jamal Willis, 1991-94

Most Rushes

Game	37	Pete Van Valkenburg vs. Utah, 11/18/72
Season	232	Van Valkenburg, 1972
Career	625	Jeff Blanc, 1973-76

Best Rushing Average

Game	13.6	Eldon Fortie vs. George Washington, 9/29/62
Season	8.64	Eddie Stinnett, 1983
	8.62	Stacey Corley, 1989
Career	5.5	Peter Tuipulotu, 1987-91
	5.2	P.VanValkenburg, 1970-72

Longest Scoring Run

	93	Weldon Jackson vs. Fresno State, 9/20/58
	92	Phil Brady vs. Utah, 1962

Longest Run From Scrimmage

	93	Weldon Jackson vs. Fresno State, 9/20/58
	92	Phil Brady, Utah, 1962

OFFENSE

Most Yards

Game	603	Ty Detmer vs. SDSU, 11/16/91
Season	5,022	Ty Detmer, 1990
	4,627	Jim McMahon, 1980
Career	14,692	Ty Detmer, 1988-91

Most Plays

Game	68	Jim McMahon vs. CSU, 11/7/81; UH, 10/25/80
	68	Robbie Bosco vs. New Mexico, 10/19/85
Season	635	Ty Detmer, 1990
Career	1,795	Ty Detmer, 1988-91

PASSING

Most Yards Passing

Game	619	John Walsh vs. Utah State, 10/30/93
Season	5,188	Ty Detmer, 1990#
Career	15,031	Ty Detmer (1988-91)#

Most Touchdown Passes

Game	7	Marc Wilson vs. CSU, 10/15/77
	7	Jim McMahon vs. CSU, 11/7/81
Season	47	Jim McMahon, 1980
Career	121	Ty Detmer, 1988-91#

Most Passes Attempted

Game	65	Jim McMahon vs. CSU, 11/7/81
Season	562	Ty Detmer, 1990
Career	1,530	Ty Detmer, 1988-91#

Most Passes Completed

Game	44	Jim McMahon vs. CSU, 11/7/81
Season	361	Ty Detmer, 1990
Career	958	Ty Detmer, 1988-91

Best Completion Percentage

Game	.911	Steve Sarkisian vs. Fresno St., 11/25/95
Season	.713	Steve Young, 1983#
Career	.672	Steve Sarkisian, 1996-96

Most Interceptions Thrown

Game	7	Jim Eccles vs. Utah, 10/9/48
Season	28	Ty Detmer, 1990
Career	65	Ty Detmer, 1988-91

Most Sacks

Game	10	Ty Detmer vs. Hawaii, 9/28/89
	10	John Walsh vs. UCLA, 9/9/93
Season	43	John Walsh, 1993
Career	108	Ty Detmer, 1988-91

Best Interception Avoidance

Season	1.7%	Jim McMahon, 1981#
Career	3.2%	Jim McMahon, 1977-81

Longest Pass Play

	97	Ty Detmer to Eric Drage vs. Utah, 11/23/91

RECEIVING

Pass Receiving

Game	22	Jay Miller vs. New Mexico, 11/3/73#
Season	100	Jay Miller, 1973
Career	204	Matt Bellini, 1987-90

Most Yards Pass Receiving

Game	263	Jay Miller vs. New Mexico, 11/3/73
Season	1,241	Andy Boyce, 1990
Career	3,066	Eric Drage, 1990-93

Most Touchdown Passes Caught

Game	4	Kirk Pendleton vs. New Mexico, 10/15/83
	4	John VanderWouden vs. CSU, 9/18/76
Season	15	Clay Brown, 1980
Career	29	Eric Drage, 1990-93

Most Yards Per Catch

Game	59	Tyler Anderson vs. Utah State, 10/30/93
Season	27.3	George Harris, 1976
Career	22.4	Lloyd Jones, 1977-80

 # NCAA Record

PASS INTERCEPTIONS

Most Pass Interceptions

Game	3	Derwin Gray vs. New Mexico, 10/27/90
	3	Jeff Wilcox vs. Wyoming, 10/18/86
	3	Tony Hernandez vs. Colorado State, 9/18/76
	3	Dave Atkinson vs. North Texas, 9/10/71
	3	Bobby Roberts vs. Texas Western, 11/5/66
	3	Gene Frantz vs. CSU, 10/6/62; UNM, 11/3/62
Season	9	Dave Atkinson, 1971
	9	Gene Frantz, 1962
Career	20	Dave Atkinson, 1971-73

Most Yards Interception Returns

Game	97	Brian Mitchell* vs. New Mexico, 9/2/89
Season	233	Dan Hansen, 1971
Career	421	Dan Hansen, 1970-72

* Longest Int. returned for a touchdown

PUNT RETURNS

Most Yards on Punt Returns

Game	219	Golden Richards vs. North Texas, 9/10/71
Season	624	Golden Richards, 1971
Career	1,312	Vai Sikahema, 1980-85

Most Punt Returns

Game	8	Don Bushore vs. Pepperdine, 11/26/49
	8	Vai Sikahema vs. New Mexico, 10/19/85
Season	54	Vai Sikahema, 1985
Career	153	Vai Sikahema, 1980-85

Best Average Punt Return

Game	79.0	James Dye vs. Utah State, 10/4/96
Season	22.9	Don Bushore, 1948
Career	19.8	James Dye, 1995-96

Most Touchdowns on Punt Returns

Game	2	Golden Richards vs. North Texas, 9/10/71#
Season	4	Golden Richards, 1971#
Career	4	James Dye, 1995-96
	4	Golden Richards, 1970-71

Longest Punt Return

Game	94	Kent Oborn vs. Arizona, 11/20/65

KICKOFF RETURNS

Most Kickoff Returns

Game	6	Stacey Corley vs. Hawaii, 12/1/90
	6	Tony Crutchfield vs. Utah, 11/19/88
Season	27	Chris Farasopoulos, 1970
Career	51	Chris Farasopoulos, 1968-70

Best Average Kickoff Returns

Game	54.5	James Dye vs. UTEP, 11/2/96
Season	40.1	Paul Allen, 1961#
Career	27.2	Chris Farasopoulos, 1968-70

Longest Kickoff Return

Game	100	James Dye vs. UTEP, 11/2/96
	100	Tyler Anderson vs. Utah State, 10/30/93
	100	Eric Mortensen vs. Utah State, 9/30/88
	100	John Betham vs. Utah, 11/23/74

COMBINED RETURNS

Most Yards

Game	247	Golden Richards vs. NTSU 9/10/71, 7 returns#
Career	2,454	Chris Farasopoulos, 1968-70

Most Returns

Game	10	Chris Farasopoulos vs. Arizona, 1969
	10	Golden Richards vs. Arizona, 1971
	10	Vai Sikahema vs. Boston College, 1985
Season	80	Chris Farasopoulos, 1970
Career	202	Vai Sikahema, 1980-85#

 # NCAA Record

PUNTING

Most Punts

Game	15	Rich Adams vs. Iowa State, 9/27/69
Season	83	Rich Adams, 1969
Career	204	Alan Boardman, 1993-96

Best Punting Average

Game	60.4	Lee Johnson vs. Wyoming, 10/8/83#
Season	50.6	Lee Johnson, 1983
Career	47.0	Lee Johnson, 1983-84

Longest Punt

	80	Lee Johnson vs. Wyoming, 10/8/83

NCAA Records

TEAM RECORDS

Both Teams Gaining 600 Yards
BYU (767) vs. SDSU (695) 11/16/91

Highest Average Per Punt
60.4 vs. Wyoming, 10/8/83
5 for 302 (min. 5)

Highest Average Per Punt, Both Teams
55.3 vs. Wyoming, 10/8/83
11 for 608 (min. 10)

Most TDs Scored On Kickoff Returns
2 vs. Air Force 11/11/89

Most Point Scored in a Tie
104 BYU (52) vs. SDSU (52), 11/16/91

Highest Average Gain per Attempt
10.9 1989, 433 for 4,732 (min. 350 att.)

Highest Average Gain Per Completion
17.0 1989, 279 for 4,732
(min. 225 comps.)

Highest Passing Efficiency
174.5 1989, 433 att., 279 comp., 15 int.,
4,732 yards, 33 TD passes
(min. 150 att.)

Team with Two 1,000-Yard Receivers
1990 Andy Boyce, 1,241; Chris Smith, 1,156

Highest Punting Average
50.6 1983, 24 for 1,215

Highest Net Punting Average
1983 45.0, 24 for 1,215 yards,
134 return yards

Most First Downs by Passing
30 BYU vs. CSU, Nov. 7, 1981

Most First Downs per Game
30.9 BYU, 1983, 340 in 11 games

Most Opponent's Fumbles Recovered
36 1977

Consecutive Games Scoring on a Pass
53 from 9/7/89 to 9/18/93

Consec. Games Passing for 200 Yards
64 9/80 to 10/19/85

Consec. Games without Being Shutout
275 10/3/75 to present

Highest-Scoring Tie Game
52-52 vs. San Diego St. 11/16/91

TOTAL OFFENSE – SINGLE GAME

Player, School (Opponent)	Yards	Rush	Pass	Date
David Klingler, Houston (ASU)	732	16	713	Dec. 2, 1990
Matt Vogler, TCU (Houston)	696	6	690	Nov. 3, 1990
David Klingler, Houston (TCU)	625	62	563	Nov. 3, 1990
Scott Mitchell, Utah (Air Force)	625	-6	631	Oct. 15, 1988
Jimmy Klingler, Houston (Rice)	612	-1	613	Nov. 28, 1992
Ty Detmer, BYU (SDSU)	**603**	**4**	**599**	**Nov. 16, 1991**
Troy Kopp, Pacific, Cal. (NMS)	601	37	564	Oct. 20, 1990
Virgil Carter, BYU (UTEP)	**599**	**86**	**513**	**Nov. 5, 1966**
John Walsh, BYU (Utah St.)	**597**	**-22**	**619**	**Oct. 30, 1993**
Jeremy Leach, UNM (Utah)	594	-28	622	Nov. 11, 1989

TOTAL OFFENSE – SEASON

Player, School	Year	G	Plays	Yards	Avg
David Klingler, Houston	*1990	11	704	5,221	7.42
Ty Detmer, BYU	**1990**	**12**	**635**	**5,022**	**7.91**
Andre Ware, Houston	*1989	11	628	4,661	7.42
Jim McMahon, BYU	***1980**	**12**	**540**	**4,627**	**8.57**
Ty Detmer, BYU	**1989**	**12**	**497**	**4,433**	**#8.92**
Steve Young, BYU	***1983**	**11**	**531**	**4,3,46**	**8.18**
Chris Vargas, Nevada	*1993	11	535	4,332	8.10
Scott Mitchell, Utah	*1988	11	589	4,299	7.03
Robbie Bosco, BYU	**1985**	**13**	**578**	**4,141**	**7.16**
Ty Detmer, BYU	**1991**	**12**	**478**	**4,001**	**8.37**

**National champion* *#Record for minimum of 3,000 yards*

SEASON PASSING YARDS

Player (School)	Year	G	Att	Cmp	Int	Pct	Yds	TD
Ty Detmer, BYU	**1990**	**12**	**562**	**361**	**28**	**.642**	***5,188**	**41**
David Klingler, UH	1990	11	*643	*374	20	.582	5,140	*54
Andre Ware, Houston	1989	11	578	365	15	.631	4,699	46
Jim McMahon, BYU	**1980**	**12**	**445**	**284**	**18**	**.638**	**4,571**	**47**
Ty Detmer, BYU	**1989**	**12**	**412**	**265**	**15**	**.643**	**4,560**	**32**
Scott Mitchell, Utah	1988	11	533	323	15	.606	4,322	29
Robbie Bosco, BYU	**1985**	**13**	**511**	**338**	**24**	**.661**	**4,273**	**30**
Chris Vargas, Nevada	1993	11	490	331	18	.676	4,265	34
Ty Detmer, BYU	**1991**	**12**	**404**	**249**	**12**	**.618**	**4,031**	**35**
Steve Sarkisian, BYU	**1996**	**14**	**404**	**278**	**12**	**.688**	**4,027**	**33**

**Record*

CAREER PASSING PER ATTEMPT

Player (School)	Year	Att	Total Cmp	Per Yds	Per Com	Att
Ty Detmer, BYU	**1988–91**	***1,530**	***958**	***15,031**	***15.7**	***9.82**
Jim McMahon, BYU	**1977–81**	**1,060**	**653**	**9,536**	***14.6**	**9.00**
Marvin Graves, Syr.	1990–93	943	563	8,466	15.0	8.89
John Walsh, BYU	**1991–94**	**973**	**587**	**8,375**	**14.3**	**8.61**
Chuck Long, Iowa	1981–85	1,072	692	9,210	13.3	8.59
Steve Young, BYU	**1981–83**	**908**	**592**	**7,733**	**13.1**	**8.52**
Robbie Bosco, BYU	**1983–85**	**997**	**638**	**8,400**	**13.2**	**8.43**
Dan McGuire, SDSU	1986–90	973	575	8,164	14.2	8.39
Doug Flutie, BC	1981–84	1,270	677	10,579	15.6	8.33
Marc Wilson, BYU	**1977–79**	**937**	**535**	**7,637**	**14.27**	**8.15**

**Record*

INDIVIDUAL NCAA RECORDS

Most Plays
3 Yrs 1,610 Ty Detmer, 1989-91, 13,456 yards
Career 1,795 Ty Detmer, 1988-91, 14,665 yards

Most Yards Gained
2 Yrs 9,455 Ty Detmer, 1989-90, -293 run, 9,748 pass
3 Yrs 13,456 Ty Detmer, 1988-90 -323 run, 13,779 pass
Career 14,665 Ty Detmer, 1988-91, -366 run, 15,031 pass

Most Seasons Gaining 4,000 yards
3 Ty Detmer, 1989-91

Most Seasons Gaining 3,000 yards
3 Ty Detmer, 1989-91

Most Seasons Gaining 2,500 yards
3 Ty Detmer, 1989-91

Most Yards Gained as a Sophomore
4,433 Ty Detmer, 1989 (12 games)

Most Games Gaining 300 Yards
Season 12 Ty Detmer, 1990
Career 33 Ty Detmer, 1988-91

Most Consecutive 300-Yard Games
Season 12 Ty Detmer, 1990
Career 19 Ty Detmer, 1989-90

Most Games Gaining 400 Yards
Career 13 Ty Detmer, 1988-91

Most Consecutive 400-Yard Games
Season 5 Ty Detmer, 1990
Career 5 Ty Detmer, 1988-91

Most Yards Against One Opponent
Career 1,483 Ty Detmer vs. SDSU, 1988-91

Yards Per Game vs. One Opponent
Career 370.8 Ty Detmer vs. SDSU,
(min. 4 games) 1988-91

Highest Average Gain Per Play
Season 8.9 Ty Detmer, 1989,
(min. 3,000 yds.) 497 for 4,433
Career 8.2 Ty Detmer, 1988-91,
(min. 7,500 yds.) 1,795 for 14,665

Highest Average Gain Per Return
Season 40.1 Paul Allen, 1961
(min. 1.2 rets. per game) 12 for 481

Most Touchdowns Responsible For
3 Yrs 122 Ty Detmer, 1989-91, 14 run, 108 pass
Career 135 Ty Detmer, 1988-91 14 run, 121 pass

Most Points Responsible For
3 Yrs 582 Ty Detmer, 1988-90 10 run, 86 pass, 3 2-pts
Career 820 Ty Detmer, 1988-91 14 run, 121 pass, 5 2-pts

Points Responsible for Per Game
2 Yrs 22.8 J.McMahon, '80-81 (502, 22)
3 Yrs 17.1 Ty Detmer, '88-90 (582, 34)
Career 17.8 Ty Detmer, '88-91 (820, 46)

Most TDs Responsible For Per Game
3 Yrs 3.4 Ty Detmer, '89-91 (122, 36)
Career 2.9 Ty Detmer, '88-91 (135, 46)

Highest Pass. Efficiency Rating
Career 162.73 Ty Detmer,1988-91
(min. 200 comp.) 1,530 att., 958 comp., 65 int., 15,031 yds., 121 TD passes

Most Catches Per Game by a Tight End
Career 5.4 Gordon Hudson, 1980-83 178 in 33 games

Most Yards Gained by a Tight End
Game 259 Gordon Hudson vs. Utah 11/21/81, 13 catches
Season 1,156 Chris Smith, BYU, 1990 68 catches
Career 2,484 Gordon Hudson, 1980-83 178 catches

Most Yards Per Game by a Tight End
Career 75.3 Gordon Hudson, 1980-83 2,484 in 33 games

Two Players Gaining 1,000 Yards
Andy Boyce 1,241 yards, 79 catches, '90
Chris Smith 1,156 yards, 68 catches, '90

Average Per Catch by a Tight End
Career 19.2 Clay Brown, 1978-80
(min. 75) 88 catches for 1,691 yards

Highest Average Per Punt
Game 60.4 Lee Johnson vs. Wyoming
(min. 5) 10/8/83 (5 for 302; 53, 63,62, 80 yards)

Most Punt Returns
Career 153 Vai Sikahema, 1980-81, 1984-85, 1,312 yds

Most TDs Scored on Punt Returns
Season 4 Golden Richards, 1971

Most TDs Scored on Kickoff Returns
Game 2 Stacey Corley vs. Air Force 11/11/89, 99 and 85 yds

Most Yards on Kick Returns
Game 247 Golden Richards vs. North Texas 9/10/71, 7 returns

Extra Points Attempted by Kicking
Season 71 Kurt Gunther, 1980, 64 of 71

Field Goals in First Game of Career
5 Joe Liljenquist vs. Colorado 9/20/69 (6 attempts)

Most Games with 200 Yards Passing
12 Steve Sarkisian, 1996

Yards Total Offense First Two Seasons
6,996 Steve Sarkisian, 1995-96

Single-Game Completion Percentage
.912 Steve Sarkisian vs. Fresno St. 11/25/95 (31 of 34 passing)

SEASON PASSING EFFICIENCY

Player (School)	Year	Att	Cmp	Int	Yds	TD	Pts
Danny Wuerffel, Florida	*1995	325	210	10	3,266	35	178.4
Jim McMahon, BYU	***1980**	**445**	**284**	**18**	**4,571**	**47**	**176.9**
Ty Detmer, BYU	***1989**	**412**	**265**	**15**	**4,560**	**32**	**175.6**
Steve Sarkisian, BYU	***1996**	**404**	**278**	**12**	**4,027**	**33**	**173.6**
Trent Dilfer, Fresno St.	*1983	333	217	4	3,276	28	173.1
Kerry Collins, Penn St.	*1994	264	176	7	2,679	21	172.9
Jerry Rhome, Tulsa	*1964	326	224	4	2,870	32	172.6
Bobby Hoying, Ohio St.	1995	303	192	11	3,023	28	170.4
Elvis Grbac, Michigan	*1991	228	152	5	1,955	24	169.0
Ty Detmer, BYU	**1991**	**403**	**249**	**12**	**4,031**	**35**	**168.5**
Steve Young, BYU	***1983**	**429**	**306**	**10**	**3,902**	**33**	**168.5**

**National champion*

CAREER PASSING EFFICIENCY

Player (School)	Year	Att	Cmp	Int	Yds	TD	Pts
Ty Detmer, BYU	**1988–91**	***1,530**	***958**	**65**	***15,031**	***121**	***162.7**
Steve Sarkisian, BYU	**1995–96**	**789**	**528**	**26**	**7,464**	**53**	**162.2**
Jim McMahon, BYU	**1977–81**	**1,060**	**653**	**34**	**9,536**	**84**	**156.9**
Steve Young, BYU	**1981–83**	**908**	**592**	**33**	**7,733**	**56**	**149.8**
Robbie Bosco, BYU	**1983–85**	**997**	**638**	**36**	**8,400**	**66**	**149.4**
Mike Maxwell, Nevada	1993–95	881	560	33	7,256	62	148.5
Chuck Long, Iowa	1981–85	1,072	692	46	9,210	64	147.8
John Walsh, BYU	1991–94	973	587	35	8,375	66	147.8
Rob Johnson, USC	1991–94	963	623	24	7,743	52	145.1
Andre Ware, Houston	1987–89	1,074	660	28	8,202	75	143.3

**Record*

Individual Top 10

TOTAL OFFENSE

Game

1.	603	Ty Detmer at S. Diego St., '91
2.	599	Virgil Carter vs. UTEP, '66
3.	597	John Walsh at Utah St., '93
4.	594	Ty Detmer vs. Penn St.,'89
5.	582	Marc Wilson vs. Utah, '77
6.	562	Ty Detmer vs. Wash. St.,'89
7.	552	Jim McMahon vs. Utah, '81
8.	540	Robbie Bosco at N. Mex., '85
9.	539	Jim McMahon at Colo. St., '81
10.	521	Ty Detmer vs. Utah St., '90

Season

1.	5,022	Ty Detmer (1990)*
2.	4,627	Jim McMahon (1980)#
3.	4,433	Ty Detmer (1989)*
4.	4,346	Steve Young (1983)*
5.	4,141	Robbie Bosco (1985)
6.	4,001	Ty Detmer (1991)
7.	3,983	Steve Sarkisian (1996)
8.	3,932	Robbie Bosco (1984)*
9.	3,580	Marc Wilson (1979)*
10.	3,507	Steve Young (1982)

Career

1.	14,665	Ty Detmer (1988–91)*
2.	9,723	Jim McMahon (1978–81)
3.	8,817	Steve Young (1981–83)
4.	8,073	Robbie Bosco (1983–85)
5.	7,736	John Walsh (1991–94)
6.	7,602	Marc Wilson (1977–79)
7.	6,996	Steve Sarkisian (1995–96)
8.	6,350	Virgil Carter (1964–66)
9.	5,388	Gifford Nielsen (1975–77)
10.	4,352	Gary Sheide (1973–74)

PASSING YARDS

Game

1.	619	John Walsh at Utah St., '93
2.	599	Ty Detmer at S. Diego St., '91
3.	585	Robbie Bosco at N. Mex., '85
4.	576	Ty Detmer vs. Penn St.,'89
5.	571	Marc Wilson vs. Utah, '77
6.	565	Jim McMahon vs. Utah, '81
7.	560	Ty Detmer vs. Utah St., '90
8.	538	Jim McMahon at Colo. St., '81
9.	537	Ty Detmer vs. Wash. St., '89
10.	536	Steve Sarkisian vs. TxA&M, '96

Season

1.	5,188	Ty Detmer (1990)#
2.	4,571	Jim McMahon (1980)#
3.	4,560	Ty Detmer (1989)*
4.	4,273	Robbie Bosco (1985)*
5.	4,031	Ty Detmer (1991)
6.	4,027	Steve Sarkisian (1996)
7.	3,902	Steve Young (1983)*
8.	3,875	Robbie Bosco (1984)*
9.	3,727	John Walsh (1993)
10.	3,712	John Walsh (1994)

Career

1.	15,031	Ty Detmer (1988–91)*
2.	9,536	Jim McMahon (1978–81)
3.	8,400	Robbie Bosco (1983–85)
4.	8,390	John Walsh (1991–94)
5.	7,733	Steve Young (1981–83)
6.	7,637	Marc Wilson (1977–79)
7.	7,394	Steve Sarkisian (1995–96)
8.	5,833	Gifford Nielsen (1975–77)
9.	5,125	Virgil Carter (1964–66)
10.	4,524	Gary Sheide (1973–74)

TOUCHDOWN PASSES

Game

1.	7	Jim McMahon at Colo. St., '81
	7	Marc Wilson at Colo. St., '77
3.	6	S. Sarkisian vs. Tex. A&M, '96
	6	Ty Detmer at S. Diego St., '91
	6	Robbie Bosco vs. Baylor, '84
	6	Steve Young vs. Utah, '83
	6	Jim McMahon vs. UTEP, '80
	6	Jim McMahon at Utah St., '81
	6	Gifford Nielsen at Utah St., '77
	6	Gary Sheide vs. New Mex., '73

Season

1.	47	Jim McMahon, 1980
2.	41	Ty Detmer, 1990
3.	35	Ty Detmer, 1991
4.	34	Steve Sarkisian, 1996
5.	33	Robbie Bosco, 1984
	33	Steve Young, 1983
7.	32	Ty Detmer, 1989
8.	30	Robbie Bosco, 1985
	30	Jim McMahon, 1981
10.	29	Marc Wilson, 1979
	29	Gifford Nielsen, 1976

Career

1.	121	Ty Detmer, 1988–91
2.	84	Jim McMahon, 1978–81
3.	66	John Walsh, 1991–94
	66	Robbie Bosco, 1983–85
5.	61	Marc Wilson, 1977–79
6.	56	Steve Young, 1980–83
7.	55	Gifford Nielsen, 1975–77
8.	54	Steve Sarkisian, 1995–96
9.	50	Virgil Carter, 1964–66
10.	45	Gary Sheide, 1973–74

RUSHING YARDS

Game

1.	272	Eldon Fortie vs. G. Wash., '62
2.	215	Jeff Blanc at Wyo., '75
3.	204	Jamal Willis vs. New Mex., '94
	204	John Ogden vs. Pacific, '66
5.	190	P. Van Valkenburg at UNM,'72
6.	184	Pete vs. Wyoming, 1972
7.	179	Jeff Blanc at Colo. St., '75
	179	Dave Chadwick vs. Mont., '48
9.	177	Lakei Heimuli at Wyo., '86
10.	176	Brian McKenzie at Utah, '96

Season

1.	1,316	Pete Van Valkenburg ('72)#
2.	1,149	Eldon Fortie (1962)*
3.	1,042	Jamal Willis (1994)
4.	1,004	Jamal Willis (1992)
5.	984	Jeff Blanc (1975)
6.	977	Brian McKenzie (1996)
7.	966	Lakei Heimuli (1986)
8.	906	John Ogden (1966)*
9.	857	Lakei Heimuli (1985)
10.	851	Casey Tiumalu (1983)

Career

1.	2,970	Jamal Willis (1991–94)
2.	2,710	Lakei Heimuli (1984–86)
3.	2,663	Jeff Blanc (1973–75)
4.	2,492	Pete VanValkenburg (1970–72)
5.	2,363	John Ogden (1964–66)
6.	1,666	Eldon Fortie (1960–62)
7.	1,580	Fred Whittingham (1984–89)
8.	1,532	Casey Tiumalu (1982–83)
9.	1,528	Peter Tuipulotu (1987–91)
10.	1,449	Weldon Jackson (1956–58)

RECEIVING YARDS

Game

1.	263	Jay Miller vs. New Mex.,'73
2.	259	Gordon Hudson vs. Utah, '81
3.	242	Phil Odle vs. UTEP, '66
4.	241	Glen Kozlowski vs. BC, '85
5.	235	Andy Boyce vs. New Mex., '90
6.	232	Eric Drage vs. Fres. St., '93
7.	230	Eric Drage at New Mex., '91
8.	225	David Mills at Air Force, '84
9.	213	Eric Drage vs. Air Force, '93
10.	203	Phil Odle vs. W. Mich., '67

Season

1.	1,241	Andy Boyce (1990)
2.	1,181	Jay Miller (1973)#
3.	1,156	Chris Smith (1990)
4.	1,093	Eric Drage (1992)
5.	1,090	Chris Smith (1989)
6.	1,039	Chuck Cutler (1988)
7.	1,023	David Mills (1984)
8.	1,018	Eric Drage (1991)
9.	1,009	Clay Brown (1980)
10.	1,008	Mark Bellini (1985)

Career

1.	3,066	Eric Drage (1990–93)
2.	2,635	Matt Bellini (1987–90)
3.	2,548	Phil Odle (1965–67)
4.	2,484	Gordon Hudson (1980–83)
5.	2,429	Mark Bellini (1983–86)
6.	2,367	Chris Smith (1988–90)
7.	2,223	Glen Kozlowski ('81–85)
8.	2,205	Mike Chronister ('76–78)
9.	1,979	Dan Plater (1978–81)
10.	1,953	Andy Boyce (1989–90)

BYU Top Marks

TOUCHDOWNS

Game

1.	5	Eric Lane at Utah State, 1979
2.	4	Kalin Hall vs. UTEP, 1993
	4	Kirk Pendleton vs. N. Mex., '83
	4	John VanDerWouden vs. CSU, '76
	4	John Ogden vs. W. Mich., '64
	4	Dick Felt at San Jose St., '52

Season

1.	16	Waymon Hamilton 14 run, 2 pass, 1981
2.	15	Clay Brown (15p, 1980)
	15	Roy Oliverson, 1951
4.	14	Ronney Jenkins (11r/3p, 1996)
	14	Jamal Willis (12r/2p, 1994)
	14	Mark Bellini (14p, 1985)
	14	Lakei Heimuli (14r, 1985)
	14	Eric Lane (10r/4p, 1980)
8.	13	Andy Boyce (13p, 1990)
	13	P. VanValkenburg (12r/1p,'72)
	13	Eldon Fortie (12r/1p, 1962)

Career

1.	39	Jamal Willis (34r/5p, '91–94)
2.	32	Lakei Heimuli (30r/2p, '84–86)
	32	Waymon Hamilton (29r/3p, '81–83)
4.	29	Eric Drage (29p, 1990–93)
5.	28	Matt Bellini (14r/14p, '87–90)

SCORING

Game

1.	30	Eric Lane at Utah State, '79
2.	24	Hema Heimuli vs. N. Mex., '94
	24	Kalin Hall vs. UTEP, 1993
	24	Kirk Pendleton vs. UNM, '83
	24	J. VanDerWouden vs. CSU, '76
	24	John Ogden vs. W. Mich., '64
	24	Dick Felt at San Jose St., '52

Season

1.	123	Ethan Pochman (1996)
2.	96	Waymon Hamilton (1981)*
3.	91	Earl Kauffman (1990)
4.	90	Clay Brown (1980)*
	90	Ray Oliverson (1951)*
6.	87	Kurt Gunther (1981)
7.	86	Leonard Chitty (1987)
	86	Eldon Fortie (1962)*
9.	85	Lee Johnson (1983)
10.	84	Ronney Jenkins (1996)
	84	Jamal Willis (1994)
	84	Mark Bellini (1985)
	84	Lakei Heimuli (1985)
	84	Eric Lane (1980)
	84	Pete VanValkenburg (1973)

** Led Conference*
 # Led Nation

Career

1.	243	Kurt Gunther (1980–82)
2.	240	Jamal Willis (1991–94)
3.	192	Lakei Heimuli (1984–86)
4.	176	Matt Bellini (1987–90)
5.	174	Eric Drage (1990–93)
	174	Jeff Blanc (1973–76)
7.	167	Lee Johnson (1983–84)
8.	162	Earl Kauffman (1988–91)
	162	Pete Van Valkenburg ('70–72)
10.	155	David Lauder (1992, 1994)

KICKING

Field Goals

1.	53	Dennis Patera at Utah St., '67
2.	52	Brent Johnson at Utah, '78
	52	Leonard Chitty at UNM, '87
4.	51	Earl Kauffman vs. Texas, '88
5.	50	Lee Johnson vs. Utah St., '83
6.	49	David Lauder at UTEP, 1994
	49	David Lauder at Notre Dame, '94
	49	Leonard Chitty vs. Utah St., '86
9.	48	Earl Kauffman at UNM, '91
	48	Leonard Chitty vs. Utah St., '87
	48	Kurt Gunther vs. Wyoming,'82

Punts

1.	80	Lee Johnson at Wyo., '83
2.	79	Ben Laverty vs. Pacific, '66
3.	78	Bill Wright at Wyoming, '61
4.	74	Earl Kauffman vs. Wyo., '89
5.	71	Pat Thompson vs. UTEP, '88
6.	70	Pat Thompson vs. Pitt., '87
7.	69	Lee Johnson vs. Baylor, '84
	69	Wayne Startin vs. Wyo., '58
9.	68	Mike Mees vs. Colo. St., '82
	68	Mike Mees at Utah, 1982

INTERCEPTIONS

Game

	3	Derwin Gray vs. N. Mex., '90
	3	Jeff Wilcox at Wyoming, '86
	3	Tony Hernandez vs. CSU, '76
	3	Dave Atkinson at N. Texas, '71
	3	Bobby Roberts vs. UTEP, '66
	3	Gene Frantz at Colo. St., '62
	3	Gene Frantz vs. N. Mex., '62

Season

1.	9	Dave Atkinson (1971)
	9	Gene Frantz (1962)
3.	8	Dave Atkinson (1972)
	8	Dan Hansen (1970)
5.	7	Jeff Wilcox (1986)
	7	Tom Holmoe (1980)
	7	Dan Hansen (1971)
	7	Bobby Roberts (1967)
	7	Bobby Roberts (1966)
	7	Carroll Johnston (1957)

Career

1.	20	Dave Atkinson (1971–73)
2.	18	Dan Hansen (1970–72)
	18	Bobby Roberts (1965–67)
4.	14	Derwin Gray (1989–92)
5.	13	Brian Mitchell (1987–90)
	13	Tom Holmoe (1979–82)
7.	12	Rodney Rice (1987–88)
	12	Scott Peterson (1985–88)
9.	11	Mike Russell (1973–74)
	11	Troy Long (1985–88)

Team Records

GENERAL OFFENSE

Most Yards Total Offense
Game 777 New Mexico, 10/15/83
Season 6.790 1990 (12 games)

Most Plays
Game 101 Utah State, 9/24/76
Season 1,004 1996 (14 games)

Best Average Total Offense
Season 584.2 1983 (11 games)

Most First Downs
Game 39 (Air Force, 1983)
Season 348 1990 (12 games)

Most First Downs Per Game
Season 30.9 1983 (11 games)

Most First Downs Rushing
Game 27 Utah, 11/22/86
Season 151 1996

Most First Downs Passing
Game 30 Colorado State, 11/7/81
Season 237 1990 (12 games)

Most Passing First Downs Per Game
Season 19.8 1990 (12 games)

RUSHING

Most Rushing Attempts
Game 77 Utah 11/22/86
Season 581 1996 (14 games)

Most Yards Rushing
Game 465 Montana, 10/25/58
Season 2,549 1996 (14 games)

PASSING

Most Yards Passing
Game 619 Utah State, 10/30/93
Season 5,379 1990 (12 games)

Most Passes Attempted
Game 65 Colorado State, 11/7/81
Season 580 1990 (12 games)

Most Passes Completed
Game 44 Colorado State, 11/7/81
Season 373 1990 (12 games)

Lowest Interception Percentage
Season 2.2 1981 (12 games)

Best Completion Percentage
Season .707 1983 (11 games)

Most Passes Had Intercepted
Game 7 Utah, 10/9/48
Season 29 1990 (12 games)

Combined Pass Completions
Game 66 BYU 33, Bowling Green 33, 9/17/83
66 BYU 38, Miami 28, 9/8/90

Percentage of Interceptions by BYU
Season 13.2 1962 (10 games)

PUNT RETURNS

Most Yards
Game 258 North Texas, 9/10/71
Season 701 1971 (11 games)

Best Average Per Return
Game 47.5 Utah State, 10/4/97
Season 28.7 1969 (28 returns)

SCORING

Most Points Scored
Game 83 Texas-El Paso, 11/1/80
Season 704 1996 (14 games)

Most Points Scored in One Half
54 Western State, 1951

Most Points Scored in Quarter (1 Team)
36 Wash. State (BYU 36–7 in 4th, 9/15/90)
Combined 49 Utah State (BYU 28–21 in 4th, 10/30/93)#

Most Points Scored in a Loss
Game 56 Utah State 58, BYU 56, 10/30/93#

Fewest Points Scored
Season 10 1922 (6 games)

KICKOFF RETURNS

Most Yards
Game 270 Utah State, 10/30/93
Season 1,322 1993 (55 returns)

Best Average Per Return
Game 41.4 Air Force, 11/11/89
Season 28.7 1969 (28 returns)

INTERCEPTIONS

Most Pass Interceptions
Game 6 Western State, 9/22/51
6 Wyoming, 10/31/70
6 UTEP, 11/26/77
Season 28 1987 (12 games)

Most Yards on Interception Returns
Game 138 UTEP, 11/26/77
Season 514 1971 (11 games)

PUNTING

Most Punts
Game 15 Iowa State, 9/27/69
Season 83 1969 (3,239 yards)

Best Punting Average
Game 60.4 Wyoming, 10/8/83)#
Season 50.6 1983 (11 games)

Best Net Punting Average
Game 56.3 Utah State, 10/29/83
Season 45.0 1983 (11 games)

ATTENDANCE

Single Game At Home

66,247	Notre Dame, 10/16/93
66,235	Miami, 9/8/90

Season at Home

440,576	1996, 7 games

Season Average at Home

66,002	1990, 6 games

Season Total

701,529	1996, 15 games

Season Average

57,419	1991, 12 games

Largest Road Crowds

96,304	Penn State, 9/21/91
80,207	Georgia, 9/11/82

Home Attendance (Season)

440,576	1996

Overall Attendance (Season)

701,529	1996

PENALTIES & FUMBLES

Most Yards Penalized

Game	219	Weber State, 9/15/79
Season	1,319	1980 (12 games)

Fewest Yards Penalized

Game	0	Four times; most recent vs. CSU, 11/13/65
Season	204	1953 (10 games)

Most Penalties

Game	22	Utah State, 10/18/80
Season	141	1980 (12 games)

Most Opponents' Fumbles Recovered

Game	7	Wichita State, 9/15/56
Season	36	1977 (11 games)

Fewest Fumbles Lost

Game	0	Many times
Season	9	1957 and 1976

DEFENSE

Lowest Defensive Yardage

Game	66	W. Michigan, 11/14/64
Season	2,381	1954 (9 games)

Lowest Average Per Game

244.5	1958 (10 games)

Fewest Rushing Yards Allowed

Game	-29	UTEP, 10/26/68
Season	874	1967 (10 games)

Lowest Rushing Per Attempt

Season	2.1	1967

Fewest Passing Yards Allowed

Game	2	New Mexico, 11/7/59
Season	605	1952 (60.5 yd per game)

Fewest First Downs Allowed

Game	3	New Mexico, 11/8/62
Season	111	1954 (9 games)

Fewest Points Allowed

Game	0	Several times; most recent Rice, 11/9/96 New Mexico, 11/7/92
Season	41	1937 (4.6 per game)

MISCELLANEOUS

Most Consecutive Wins in a Season

13	1984

Most Consecutive Wins

25	1983–85

Most Games Without Being Shutout

260	1975–present

Most Games Without a Tie

219	1974–91

Consecutive Games With a TD Pass

53	1989–93

Fewest First Downs

Game	4	Wichita State, 9/15/56
	4	Iowa State, 9/27/69
Season	105	1961

Poorest Offensive Yards

Game	42	Iowa State, 9/27/69
Season	105	1961

Poorest Rushing Offense

Game	–96	New Mexico, 11/14/70
Season	1,061	1995

Poorest Passing Offense

Game	9	Iowa State, 9/27/69
	9	Tulsa, 11/23/71

Terrence Harvey
1976–1997

IN MEMORY